Differentiated Instruction
Teacher Management System

HOLT McDOUGAL

United States Government
Principles in Practice

HOLT McDOUGAL
a division of Houghton Mifflin Harcourt

ISBN-13: 978-0-55-401055-7
ISBN-10: 0-55-401055-0

1 2 3 4 5 6 7 170 12 11 10 09 08

Contents

Teacher Management System

Lesson Plans for
Differentiated Instruction

Foundations of Democracy

Interactive Reader and
Study Guide

Spanish/English Interactive
Reader and Study Guide

The ***Differentiated Instruction Teacher Management System*** includes a number of valuable tools that will help you use the resources provided with *Holt McDougal United States Government: Principles in Practice* to their fullest extent. With the approaches in this book, you will be able to provide innovative and varied strategies for helping students master the material, tailor your instruction to the special needs and abilities of your students, and thoroughly assess how well each student is mastering the concepts and information in the textbook. Included in this book are the following:

- Semester and Yearly Pacing Guides
- Section Lesson Plans
- Lesson Plans for Differentiated Instruction
- Teaching Guide and Answer Key for Foundations of Democracy
- Teaching Guide and Answer Key for Interactive Reader and Study Guide
- Teaching Guide and Answer Key for Spanish/English Interactive Reader and Study Guide

Used together, these tools will enable you to help your students get the most from *Holt McDougal United States Government: Principles in Practice*, gaining a full understanding and appreciation of the functions of our government.

SEMESTER AND YEARLY PACING GUIDES

The Semester Pacing Guide and Yearly Pacing Guide provide detailed time lines of how much time each section and chapter is expected to take. The Semester Pacing Guide is based on a single, 16-week semester. The Yearly Pacing Guide is based on a 30-week year.

SECTION LESSON PLANS

The Section Lesson Plans provide a basic planning form to help you organize your lessons for each section in the textbook. The form includes check-off lines so that you can mark which items and resources you plan to use. The Section Lesson Plans include:

- **Objectives** A repeat of the section's Main Idea and Reading Focus, which are located at the start of each section in the Student Edition;
- **Key Terms** A list of the section's vocabulary terms;
- **Resources** A list of the resources available for each part of the lesson;
- **Lesson Plan Organization** An instructional plan organized according to the Teacher's Edition lesson cycle.

LESSON PLANS FOR DIFFERENTIATED INSTRUCTION

The Lesson Plans for Differentiated Instruction component offers strategies for teaching students with special needs. These strategies are designed to help students meet benchmarks and master the most important information and concepts. The lesson plans provide differentiated instruction for the following categories:

- English-Language Instruction
- Special Education Instruction
- Advanced/Gifted and Talented Instruction

Each Lesson Plan for Differentiated Instruction includes side notes that link to a specific strategy or support differentiated instruction for that section in general. The side notes include examples of graphic organizers—charts, Venn diagrams, flow charts, tables, and concept webs—and a list of resources available for each chapter of the book. Also included are Teacher Tips to give you additional tools for instruction, Vocabulary Tips that include additional information about terms found in the chapter, and Technology Tips that provide Web sites related to the material.

TEACHING GUIDE AND ANSWER KEY FOR FOUNDATIONS OF DEMOCRACY

The Center for Civic Education's *Foundations of Democracy* is a student resource designed to help students examine the fundamental values of our government. Organized around the concepts of authority, privacy, responsibility, and justice, *Foundations of Democracy* challenges students to think for themselves, to develop reasoned positions, and to articulate and defend their views.

The Teaching Tips and Answer Key includes answers to selected Critical Thinking Exercises and other questions from *Foundations of Democracy*. Also included are strategies for incorporating each lesson in your classroom instruction. The Teaching Tips and Answer Key section is organized by lesson.

TEACHING GUIDE AND ANSWER KEY FOR INTERACTIVE READER AND STUDY GUIDE

The *Interactive Reader and Study Guide* provides a graphic summary of each chapter, followed by comprehension and critical thinking questions related to the chapter material. In addition, the *Interactive Reader and Study Guide* provides a replication of the Taking Notes graphic organizer that appears in each section of the student edition. The *Interactive Reader and Study Guide* also presents each section's main idea, its key terms, and a summary with side-margin questions.

The goal of the *Interactive Reader and Study Guide* is to provide assistance for students who are having problems accessing the concepts that they must master for standards, testing, and other assessment. The workbook is a student consumable and does not include answers. Answers for the *Interactive Reader and Study Guide*, along with a brief Teachers Guide, are provided in the *Interactive Reader and Study Guide* portion of this book.

TEACHING GUIDE AND ANSWER KEY FOR SPANISH/ENGLISH INTERACTIVE READER AND STUDY GUIDE

The *Spanish/English Interactive Reader and Study Guide* provides each section's graphic organizer, main idea, key terms, summary with side-margin interactive instructional support, and section assessment in both Spanish and English. This core content is organized so that small chunks, or sections, of the content are provided in both Spanish and English for easy translation.

The goal of the *Spanish/English Interactive Reader and Study* Guide is to provide assistance for English-Language Learners. The workbook should help students understand the important points of each section and be prepared to pass chapter and unit assessments. The workbook is a student consumable and does not include answers. Answers in both Spanish and English, along with a brief Teachers Guide, are provided in the *Spanish/English Interactive Reader and Study Guide* portion of this book.

Pacing Guides

TIME	LESSON AND ACTIVITY (NUMBER OF 45-MINUTE CLASS PERIODS)
Week 1	**HOLT MCDOUGAL UNITED STATES GOVERNMENT: PRINCIPLES IN PRACTICE** **Part 1: Essentials of United States Government** *(55)* **Chapter 1:** Foundations of Government *(5)* **Section 1:** The Purposes of Government (1) **Section 2:** Forms of Government (1) **Section 3:** Democracy in the United States (1) • Landmark Supreme Court Case: *Gideon* v. *Wainwright* (1963) **We the People:** Constitutional Government (1) Chapter Review (1)
Weeks 2–3	**Chapter 2:** Origins of American Government *(6)* **Section 1:** The Roots of American Democracy (1) **Section 2:** American Independence (1) **Section 3:** Articles of Confederation (1) **Section 4:** The Constitutional Convention (1) **Section 5:** Ratification and the Bill of Rights (1) • Landmark Supreme Court Case: *Schenck* v. *United States* (1919) **We the People**: Individual Rights and the U.S. Constitution (1/2) Chapter Review (1/2)
Week 3	**Chapter 3:** The Constitution *(4)* **Section 1:** A Blueprint for Government (1) • Landmark Supreme Court Case: *Marbury* v. *Madison* (1803) **Section 2:** An Enduring Document (1) **Section 3:** Applying the Constitution (1) **We the People:** A New Constitution and a New Government (1/2) Chapter Review (1/2)
Week 4	**Chapter 4:** Federalism *(4)* **Section 1:** Dividing Government Power (1) **Section 2:** American Federalism: Conflict and Change (1) • Landmark Supreme Court Case: *McCulloch* v. *Maryland* (1819) **Section 3:** Federalism Today (1) **We the People:** Laboratories of Democracy (1/2) Chapter Review (1/2)

TIME	LESSON AND ACTIVITY (NUMBER OF 45-MINUTE CLASS PERIODS)
Weeks 4–5	**Chapter 5:** Congress: The Legislative Branch *(6)* **Section 1:** Congress (1) **Section 2:** The Powers of Congress (1) • Landmark Supreme Court Case: *Gibbons* v. *Ogden* (1824) **Section 3:** The House of Representatives (1) **Section 4:** The Senate (1) **Section 5:** Congress at Work (1) **We the People:** The Sources of Laws (1/2) Chapter Review (1/2)
Week 6	**Chapter 6:** The Presidency *(5)* **Section 1:** The President (1) **Section 2:** The Powers of the Presidency (1) • Landmark Supreme Court Case: *United States* v. *Nixon* (1974) **Section 3:** The President's Administration (1) **We the People:** Executive Power and the President (1) Chapter Review (1)
Week 7	**Chapter 7:** The Executive Branch at Work *(5)* **Section 1:** The Federal Bureaucracy (1) **Section 2:** Executive Departments and Independent Agencies (1) • Landmark Supreme Court Case: *Schechter Poultry Corporation* v. *United States* (1935) **Section 3:** Financing Government (1) **We the People:** The Federal Bureaucracy (1) Chapter Review (1)
Week 8	**Chapter 8:** The Federal Courts and the Judicial Branch *(5)* **Section 1:** The Federal Court System (1) **Section 2:** Lower Federal Courts (1) **Section 3:** The Supreme Court (1) • Landmark Supreme Court Case: *Plessy* v. *Ferguson* (1896) **We the People:** The Supreme Court and the System of Checks and Balances (1) Chapter Review (1)
Week 9	**Chapter 9:** The Political Process *(5)* **Section 1:** Public Opinion (1) **Section 2:** Interest Groups (1) **Section 3:** Political Parties (1) **Section 4:** The Electoral Process (1) • Landmark Supreme Court Case: *Buckley* v. *Valeo* (1976) **We the People:** Role of Political Parties in the Constitutional System (1/2) Chapter Review (1/2)

TIME	LESSON AND ACTIVITY (NUMBER OF 45-MINUTE CLASS PERIODS)
Week 10	**Chapter 10:** Civil Liberties *(5)* **Section 1:** Protecting Constitutional Rights (1) **Section 2:** First Amendment Freedoms (1) **Section 3:** Protecting Individual Liberties (1) **Section 4:** Crime and Punishment (1) • Landmark Supreme Court Case: *Miranda* v. *Arizona* (1966) **We the People:** Fundamental Rights and the Doctrine of Incorporation (1/2) Chapter Review (1/2)

Week 11	**Chapter 11:** Civil Rights *(5)*
	Section 1: Civil Rights and Discrimination (1)
	Section 2: Equal Justice under Law (1)
	  • Landmark Supreme Court Case: *Brown* v. *Board of Education of*
	    Topeka, Kansas (1954)
	Section 3: Civil Rights Laws (1)
	Section 4: Citizenship and Immigration (1)
	We the People: Civic Participation (1/2)
	Chapter Review (1/2)

Week 12	**Part 2: Interactive United States Government** *(25)*
	Chapter 12: Understanding Elections *(5)*
	Section 1: Election Campaigns (1)
	  • Simulation: Running a Presidential Campaign
	Section 2: Campaign Funding and Political Action Committees (1)
	  • Simulation: Deciding to Back a Candidate
	Section 3: Election Day and the Voters (2)
	  • Simulation: Planning Election Day Strategies
	Chapter Review (1)

Week 13	**Chapter 13:** Supreme Court Cases *(5)*
	Section 1: The First Amendment: Your Freedom of Expression (1)
	  • Simulation: The Play's the Thing
	Section 2: The Fourth Amendment: Your Right to Be Secure (1)
	  • Simulation: Have You Been Seized?
	Section 3: Due Process and the Fourteenth Amendment (1)
	  • Simulation: Terrorists and Due Process
	Section 4: Federalism and the Supreme Court (1)
	  • Simulation: Arguing a Federalism Case
	Chapter Review (1)

TIME	LESSON AND ACTIVITY (NUMBER OF 45-MINUTE CLASS PERIODS)
Week 14	**Chapter 14:** Making Foreign Policy *(5)* **Section 1:** Foreign Policy Choices in a Complex World (1) • Simulation: Deciding Whether to Use Military Intervention **Section 2:** How Domestic Actors Affect Foreign Policy (1) • Simulation: Senate Trade Bill Vote **Section 3:** Foreign Policy and International Institutions (1) • Simulation: Crisis at the UN Security Council **Section 4:** Foreign Policy Challenges (1) • Simulation: Negotiating an Environmental Treaty Chapter Review (1)
Week 15	**Chapter 15:** Comparative Political and Economic Systems *(5)* **Section 1:** Democratic Governments (1) • Simulation: Choosing a System of Government **Section 2:** Authoritarian Governments (1) • Simulation: Overthrowing a Dictator **Section 3:** Economic Systems (2) • Simulation: Negotiating a Trade Agreement Chapter Review (1)
Week 16	**Chapter 16:** State and Local Government *(5)* **Section 1:** States and the National Government (1) • Simulation: Amending the State Constitution **Section 2:** State Government (2) • Simulation: Budgeting and Public Policy **Section 3:** Local Government and Citizen Participation (1) • Simulation: Conducting the City's Business Chapter Review (1)

Additional Teacher Resources to Support **Intervention and Differentiated Instruction**
  • Interactive Reader and Study Guide
  • Spanish/English Interactive Reader and Study Guide
  • Guided Reading Activities with Answer Key
  • Teaching Transparencies
  • Advanced Placement Review and Activities with Answer Key
  • Differentiated Instruction Modified Worksheets and Tests on the Teacher One Stop™

TIME	LESSON AND ACTIVITY (NUMBER OF 45-MINUTE CLASS PERIODS)
Weeks 1–2	**HOLT UNITED STATES GOVERNMENT: PRINCIPLES IN PRACTICE** **Part 1: Essentials of United States Government** *(100)* **Chapter 1:** Foundations of Government *(8)* Section 1: The Purposes of Government (2) Section 2: Forms of Government (2) Section 3: Democracy in the United States (2) • Landmark Supreme Court Case: *Gideon* v. *Wainwright* (1963) **We the People:** Constitutional Government (1) Chapter Review (1)
Weeks 2–4	**Chapter 2:** Origins of American Government *(10)* Section 1: The Roots of American Democracy (1) Section 2: American Independence (2) Section 3: Articles of Confederation (1) Section 4: The Constitutional Convention (2) Section 5: Ratification and the Bill of Rights (2) • Landmark Supreme Court Case: *Schenck* v. *United States* (1919) **We the People**: Individual Rights and the U.S. Constitution (1) Chapter Review (1)
Weeks 5–6	**Chapter 3:** The Constitution *(10)* Section 1: A Blueprint for Government (2) • Landmark Supreme Court Case: *Marbury* v. *Madison* (1803) Section 2: An Enduring Document (3) Section 3: Applying the Constitution (3) **We the People:** A New Constitution and a New Government (1) Chapter Review (1)
Weeks 6–7	**Chapter 4:** Federalism *(7)* Section 1: Dividing Government Power (2) Section 2: American Federalism: Conflict and Change (2) • Landmark Supreme Court Case: *McCulloch* v. *Maryland* (1819) Section 3: Federalism Today (1) **We the People:** Laboratories of Democracy (1) Chapter Review (1)

TIME	LESSON AND ACTIVITY (NUMBER OF 45-MINUTE CLASS PERIODS)
Weeks 7–9	**Chapter 5**: Congress: The Legislative Branch *(15)* **Section 1:** Congress (3) **Section 2:** The Powers of Congress (3) • Landmark Supreme Court Case: *Gibbons* v. *Ogden* (1824) **Section 3:** The House of Representatives (2) **Section 4:** The Senate (2) **Section 5:** Congress at Work (3) **We the People:** The Sources of Laws (1) Chapter Review (1)
Weeks 10–11	**Chapter 6**: The Presidency *(8)* **Section 1:** The President (2) **Section 2:** The Powers of the Presidency (2) • Landmark Supreme Court Case: *United States* v. *Nixon* (1974) **Section 3:** The President's Administration (2) **We the People:** Executive Power and the President (1) Chapter Review (1)
Weeks 11–12	**Chapter 7**: The Executive Branch at Work *(7)* **Section 1:** The Federal Bureaucracy (2) **Section 2:** Executive Departments and Independent Agencies (2) • Landmark Supreme Court Case: *Schechter Poultry Corporation* v. *United States* (1935) **Section 3:** Financing Government (1) **We the People:** The Federal Bureaucracy (1) Chapter Review (1)
Weeks 13–14	**Chapter 8**: The Federal Courts and the Judicial Branch *(10)* **Section 1:** The Federal Court System (3) **Section 2:** Lower Federal Courts (2) **Section 3:** The Supreme Court (3) • Landmark Supreme Court Case: *Plessy* v. *Ferguson* (1896) **We the People:** The Supreme Court and the System of Checks and Balances (1) Chapter Review (1)
Weeks 15–16	**Chapter 9**: The Political Process *(7)* **Section 1:** Public Opinion (1) **Section 2:** Interest Groups (1) **Section 3:** Political Parties (1) **Section 4:** The Electoral Process (2) • Landmark Supreme Court Case: *Buckley* v. *Valeo* (1976) **We the People:** Role of Political Parties in the Constitutional System (1) Chapter Review (1)

TIME	LESSON AND ACTIVITY (NUMBER OF 45-MINUTE CLASS PERIODS)
Weeks 16–19	**Chapter 10:** Civil Liberties *(10)* **Section 1:** Protecting Constitutional Rights (2) **Section 2:** First Amendment Freedoms (2) **Section 3:** Protecting Individual Liberties (2) **Section 4:** Crime and Punishment (2) • Landmark Supreme Court Case: *Miranda* v. *Arizona* (1966) **We the People:** Fundamental Rights and the Doctrine of Incorporation (1) Chapter Review (1)
Weeks 19–20	**Chapter 11:** Civil Rights *(8)* **Section 1:** Civil Rights and Discrimination (2) **Section 2:** Equal Justice under Law (2) • Landmark Supreme Court Case: *Brown* v. *Board of Education of Topeka, Kansas* (1954) **Section 3:** Civil Rights Laws (1) **Section 4:** Citizenship and Immigration (1) **We the People:** Civic Participation (1) Chapter Review (1)
Weeks 21–22	**Part 2: Interactive United States Government** *(50)* **Chapter 12:** Understanding Elections *(10)* **Section 1:** Election Campaigns (3) • Simulation: Running a Presidential Campaign **Section 2:** Campaign Funding and Political Action Committees (3) • Simulation: Deciding to Back a Candidate **Section 3:** Election Day and the Voters (3) • Simulation: Planning Election Day Strategies Chapter Review (1)
Weeks 23–24	**Chapter 13:** Supreme Court Cases *(10)* **Section 1:** The First Amendment: Your Freedom of Expression (3) • Simulation: The Play's the Thing **Section 2:** The Fourth Amendment: Your Right to Be Secure (2) • Simulation: Have You Been Seized? **Section 3:** Due Process and the Fourteenth Amendment (2) • Simulation: Terrorists and Due Process **Section 4:** Federalism and the Supreme Court (2) • Simulation: Arguing a Federalism Case Chapter Review (1)

TIME	LESSON AND ACTIVITY (NUMBER OF 45-MINUTE CLASS PERIODS)
Weeks 25–26	**Chapter 14:** Making Foreign Policy **(10)** **Section 1:** Foreign Policy Choices in a Complex World (2) • Simulation: Deciding Whether to Use Military Intervention **Section 2:** How Domestic Actors Affect Foreign Policy (2) • Simulation: Senate Trade Bill Vote **Section 3:** Foreign Policy and International Institutions (3) • Simulation: Crisis at the UN Security Council **Section 4:** Foreign Policy Challenges (2) • Simulation: Negotiating an Environmental Treaty Chapter Review (1)
Weeks 27–28	**Chapter 15:** Comparative Political and Economic Systems **(10)** **Section 1:** Democratic Governments (3) • Simulation: Choosing a System of Government **Section 2:** Authoritarian Governments (3) • Simulation: Overthrowing a Dictator **Section 3:** Economic Systems (3) • Simulation: Negotiating a Trade Agreement Chapter Review (1)
Week 29–30	**Chapter 16:** State and Local Government **(10)** **Section 1:** States and the National Government (3) • Simulation: Amending the State Constitution **Section 2:** State Government (3) • Simulation: Budgeting and Public Policy **Section 3:** Local Government and Citizen Participation (3) • Simulation: Conducting the City's Business Chapter Review (1)

Additional Teacher Resources to Support **Intervention and Differentiated Instruction**
  • Interactive Reader and Study Guide
  • Spanish/English Interactive Reader and Study Guide
  • Guided Reading Activities with Answer Key
  • Teaching Transparencies
  • Advanced Placement Review and Activities with Answer Key
  • Differentiated Instruction Modified Worksheets and Tests on the Teacher One Stop™

Section Lesson Plans

Foundations of Government

Lesson Plan

Section 1

Objectives Students will learn . . . 1. what government is. 2. which major characteristics all states share. 3. the major functions of government. 4. what theories of rule have been put forth to explain government. **Key Terms** Preteach the following terms: government, power, policy, state, sovereignty, politics, legitimacy, divine right of kings, social contract theory	**Teacher Notes**

PRETEACH	**RESOURCES**
___ **Before You Read . . .** (SE) Preview the Main Idea, Reading Focus, and Key Terms. ___ **Academic Vocabulary** (SE) Review with students the high-use academic term in this section.	___ CRF: Vocabulary Builder: Section 1 ___ Teacher One Stop™: Differentiated Instruction Modified Worksheets and Tests

DIRECT TEACH	**RESOURCES**
___ **Teach the Main Idea Activity** (TE) Students discuss the Reading Focus questions and write definitions for key terms in the section. ___ **Differentiating Instruction: Special Needs Learners** (TE) Branches of Government **[Below Level]** ___ **Skills Focus** (TE) Sovereign States ___ **Skills Focus** (TE) Necessary or Optional Government Functions? ___ **Collaborative Learning** (TE) Ruling Theories ___ **Collaborative Learning** (TE) Creating a Social Contract ___ **Debating the Issue** (TE, SE) Eminent Domain: Public Good over Private Property	___ Interactive Reader and Study Guide: Sec. 1 ___ Transparency: Quick Facts: Functions of Government ___ CRF: Primary Source: John Locke, *Second Treatise on Government* ___ CRF: Biographies: Thomas Hobbes and Jean Jacques Rousseau ___ CRF: Political Cartoon: Eminent Domain

REVIEW & ASSESS	**RESOURCES**
___ **Close** (TE) Have each student write a paragraph explaining what government is and why it is important. ___ **Section 1 Assessment** (SE)	___ Online Quiz Section 1 keyword: SGO FND HP ___ PASS: Section 1 Quiz

Key: SE = Student Edition **TE** = Teacher's Edition **CRF** = Chapter Resource File

Foundations of Government

Lesson Plan

Section 2

Objectives Students will learn . . .	Teacher Notes
1. the classic forms of government.	
2. how national power can be organized in unitary, federal, and confederal systems.	
3. the ways in which presidential and parliamentary systems differ.	
Key Terms Preteach the following terms: monarchy, dictatorship, oligarchy, direct democracy, republic, unitary system, federal system, confederal system, presidential system, parliamentary system	

PRETEACH	**RESOURCES**
___ **Before You Read . . .** (SE) Preview the Main Idea, Reading Focus, and Key Terms.	___ CRF: Vocabulary Builder: Section 2
	___ Teacher One Stop™: Differentiated Instruction Modified Worksheets and Tests

DIRECT TEACH	**RESOURCES**
___ **Teach the Main Idea Activity** (TE) Students discuss the Reading Focus questions and identify the classic forms of government and their characteristics.	___ Interactive Reader and Study Guide: Section 2
___ **Differentiating Instruction: Struggling Readers** (TE) Illustrating Forms of Government **[Below Level]**	___ Spanish/English Interactive Reader and Study Guide: Section 2
___ **Critical Thinking** (TE) Democracies and Dictatorships	
___ **Interpreting Charts** (SE) Power in Three Systems of Government	
___ **Critical Thinking** (TE) Organizing National Power	
___ **Collaborative Learning** (TE) Presidents and Prime Ministers	
___ **Interpreting Charts** (SE) Presidential and Primary Systems	

REVIEW & ASSESS	**RESOURCES**
___ **Close** (TE) Have students discuss forms of government that have developed through the centuries.	___ Online Quiz Section 2 keyword: SGO FND HP
___ **Section 2 Assessment** (SE)	
	___ PASS: Section 2 Quiz

Key: SE = Student Edition **TE** = Teacher's Edition **CRF** = Chapter Resource Files

Foundations of Government

Lesson Plan
Section 3

Objectives Students will learn . . .	**Teacher Notes**
1. why the ideals of liberty, equality, and self-government are important to American democracy.	
2. the principles of American democracy.	
3. why the free enterprise system is important to American democracy.	
Key Terms Preteach the following terms: ideal, liberty, equality, self-government, majority rule, minority rights, liberal democracy, free enterprise	

PRETEACH	**RESOURCES**
___ **Before You Read . . .** (SE) Preview the Main Idea, Reading Focus, and Key Terms.	___ CRF: Vocabulary Builder: Section 3
___ **Academic Vocabulary** (SE) Review with students the high-use academic term in this section.	___ Teacher One Stop™: Differentiated Instruction Modified Worksheets and Tests

DIRECT TEACH	**RESOURCES**
___ **Teach the Main Idea Activity** (TE) Students discuss the Reading Focus questions and create an outline of the section.	___ Interactive Reader and Study Guide: Section 3
___ **Critical Thinking** (TE) American Ideals	___ Spanish/English Interactive Reader and Study Guide: Section 3
___ **Primary Sources** (SE) Democracy in America	
___ **Skills Focus** (TE) America through the Eyes of Others	___ CRF: Primary Source: Tocqueville, *Democracy in America*
___ **Critical Thinking** (TE) Citizenship Essays	
___ **Landmark Supreme Court Cases** (SE) *Gideon* v. *Wainwright* (1963)	___ CRF: Economics and Government: GDP and the Public Good
___ **Collaborative Learning** (TE) The Right to Counsel	___ Supreme Court Case Studies: *Gideon* v. *Wainwright*
___ **We the People** (TE, SE) Constitutional Government	

REVIEW & ASSESS	**RESOURCES**
___ **Close** (TE) Have students discuss the core ideals and principles of American democracy.	___ Online Quiz Section 3 keyword: SGO FND HP
___ **Section 3 Assessment** (SE)	___ PASS: Section 3 Quiz

Key: SE = Student Edition **TE** = Teacher's Edition **CRF** = Chapter Resource File

Origins of American Government

Lesson Plan

Section 1

	Teacher Notes
Objectives Students will learn . . . 1. which American political ideas are derived from an English political heritage. 2. how colonial government gave English colonists experience in self-rule. 3. what intellectual influences shaped the development of American political philosophy. **Key Terms** Preteach the following terms: bicameral, Magna Carta, Petition of Right, English Bill of Rights, Fundamental Orders of Connecticut, proprietary colony, royal colonies, charter colonies	

PRETEACH	**RESOURCES**
___ **Before You Read . . .** (SE) Preview the Main Idea, Reading Focus, and Key Terms. ___ **Academic Vocabulary** (SE) Review with students the high-use academic term in this section.	___ CRF: Vocabulary Builder: Section 1 ___ Teacher One Stop™: Differentiated Instruction Modified Worksheets and Tests

DIRECT TEACH	**RESOURCES**
___ **Teach the Main Idea Activity** (TE) Students discuss the Reading Focus questions and write the main ideas and supporting details for each main heading. ___ **Collaborative Learning** (TE) A Bicameral Parliament ___ **Differentiating Instruction: Special Needs Learners** (TE) American Freedoms [Below Level] ___ **Map** (SE) Thirteen Colonies, 1750 ___ **Differentiating Instruction: Advanced/Gifted and Talented** (TE) Researching Royal Colonies [Above Level]	___ Interactive Reader and Study Guide: Section 1 ___ Transparency: Quick Facts: Important English Ideas ___ CRF: Biography: Montesquieu ___ CRF: Primary Source: Montesquieu, *Spirit of the Laws*

REVIEW & ASSESS	**RESOURCES**
___ **Close** (TE) Review with the students the different influences on the Framers and how these influences built on one another through history. ___ **Section 1 Assessment** (SE)	___ Online Quiz Section 1 keyword: SGO ORI HP ___ PASS: Section 1 Quiz

Key: SE = Student Edition **TE** = Teacher's Edition **CRF** = Chapter Resource File

Origins of American Government

Objectives Students will learn . . .	**Teacher Notes**
1. how British colonial policies led to American Independence.	
2. the aims of the Continental Congresses.	
3. which ideas and events inspired the Declaration of Independence.	
4. how the first state governments reflected the conflict that led to the American Revolution.	
Key Terms Preteach the following terms: New England Confederation, Iroquois Confederation, Albany Plan of Union, Stamp Act, First Continental Congress, Second Continental Congress, Virginia Declaration of Rights	

PRETEACH	**RESOURCES**
___ **Before You Read . . .** (SE) Preview the Main Idea, Reading Focus, and Key Terms.	___ CRF: Vocabulary Builder: Section 2
___ **Academic Vocabulary** (SE) Review with students the high-use academic term in this section.	___ Teacher One Stop™: Differentiated Instruction Modified Worksheets and Tests

DIRECT TEACH	**RESOURCES**
___ **Teach the Main Idea Activity** (TE) Students discuss the Reading Focus questions and summarize the events that led to the American Revolution.	___ Interactive Reader and Study Guide: Section 2
___ **Skills Focus** (TE) The Albany Plan of Union	___ Spanish/English Interactive Reader and Study Guide: Section 2
___ **Critical Thinking** (TE) Using Power Wisely	
___ **Differentiating Instruction: English-Language Learners** (TE) The Boston Tea Party **[Below Level]**	___ CRF: Economics and Government: War and Taxes
___ **Profiles in Government** (SE) Thomas Jefferson	
___ **Differentiating Instruction: Special Needs Learners** (TE) Declaration of Independence **[Below Level]**	
___ **Primary Source** (TE, SE) Declaration of Independence	

REVIEW & ASSESS	**RESOURCES**
___ **Close** (TE) Review with students the events leading up to the Declaration of Independence and the major concepts in this document.	___ Online Quiz Section 2 keyword: SGO ORI HP
___ **Section 2 Assessment** (SE)	___ PASS: Section 2 Quiz

Key: SE = Student Edition **TE** = Teacher's Edition **CRF** = Chapter Resource File

Origins of American Government

Lesson Plan

Section 3

Objectives Students will learn . . . 1. how the first national government was organized under the Articles of Confederation. 2. the weaknesses of the Articles of Confederation. 3. what events convinced American leaders that a stronger national government was needed. **Key Terms** Preteach the following terms: Articles of Confederation, ratified, Northwest Ordinance, Shays's Rebellion.	**Teacher Notes**
PRETEACH	**RESOURCES**
___ **Before You Read . . .** (SE) Preview the Main Idea, Reading Focus, and Key Terms. ___ **Academic Vocabulary** (SE) Review with students the high-use academic term in this section.	___ CRF: Vocabulary Builder: Section 3 ___ Teacher One Stop™: Differentiated Instruction Modified Worksheets and Tests
DIRECT TEACH	**RESOURCES**
___ **Teach the Main Idea Activity** (TE) Students discuss the Reading Focus questions and create oral presentations based on the main ideas of each main heading. ___ **Differentiating Instruction: Struggling Readers** (TE) Examining Taxes **[Below Level]** ___ **Skills Focus** (TE) Confederation or Strong Central Government?	___ Interactive Reader and Study Guide: Section 3 ___ Spanish/English Interactive Reader and Study Guide: Section 3 ___ Transparency: Quick Facts: Congress under the Articles of Confederation ___ CRF: Primary Source: Northwest Ordinance of 1787
REVIEW & ASSESS	**RESOURCES**
___ **Close** (TE) Have students review the powers that the Confederation was lacking and draw a chart listing these weaknesses and their resulting problems. ___ **Section 3 Assessment** (SE)	___ Online Quiz Section 3 keyword: SGO ORI HP ___ PASS: Section 3 Quiz

Key: SE = Student Edition **TE** = Teacher's Edition **CRF** = Chapter Resource File

Origins of American Government

Lesson Plan

Section 4

Objectives Students will learn . . . 1. why the Constitutional Convention drafted a new plan for government. 2. how rival plans at the Constitutional Convention differed. 3. what conflicts required the Framers to compromise during the Constitutional Convention. **Key Terms** Preteach the following terms: Framers, Virginia plan, New Jersey Plan, Great Compromise, Three-Fifths Compromise	**Teacher Notes**
PRETEACH	**RESOURCES**
____ **Before You Read . . .** (SE) Preview the Main Idea, Reading Focus, and Key Terms.	____ CRF: Vocabulary Builder: Section 4 ____ Teacher One Stop™: Differentiated Instruction Modified Worksheets and Tests
DIRECT TEACH	**RESOURCES**
____ **Teach the Main Idea Activity** (TE) Students discuss the Reading Focus questions and identify the major issues on which the Framers had to compromise during the Constitutional Convention. ____ **Skills Focus** (TE) Constitutional Convention ____ **Profiles in Government** (SE) James Madison ____ **Critical Thinking** (TE) Supporting a Plan ____ **Differentiating Instruction: Struggling Readers** (TE) Reviewing Constitutional Compromises **[Below Level]** ____ **Debating the Issue** (TE, SE) Mandatory national Public Service	____ Interactive Reader and Study Guide: Section 4 ____ Spanish/English Interactive Reader and Study Guide: Section 4 ____ Transparency: Quick Facts: Framers of the Constitution ____ Transparency: Quick Facts: The Great Compromise ____ CRF: Biography: Benjamin Franklin
REVIEW & ASSESS	**RESOURCES**
____ **Close** (TE) Have students review the major disagreements of the Constitutional Convention and the resolution for each. ____ **Section 4 Assessment** (SE)	____ Online Quiz Section 4 keyword: SGO ORI HP ____ PASS: Section 4 Quiz

Key: SE = Student Edition **TE** = Teacher's Edition **CRF** = Chapter Resource File

Origins of American Government   Lesson Plan

Objectives Students will learn . . .	**Teacher Notes**
1. what the main points of disagreement were between the Antifederalists and the Federalists.	
2. what main arguments were made by the authors of the *Federalist Papers*.	
3. why the Bill of Rights was important to the ratification of the Constitution.	
Key Terms Preteach the following terms: Federalists, Antifederalists, Publius, *Federalist Papers*, Bill of Rights	
PRETEACH	**RESOURCES**
___ **Before You Read . . .** (SE) Preview the Main Idea, Reading Focus, and Key Terms.	___ CRF: Vocabulary Builder: Section 5
	___ Teacher One Stop™: Differentiated Instruction Modified Worksheets and Tests
DIRECT TEACH	**RESOURCES**
___ **Teach the Main Idea Activity** (TE) Students discuss the Reading Focus questions and identify the major objections against the Constitution.	___ Interactive Reader and Study Guide: Section 5
___ **Differentiating Instruction: Struggling Readers** (TE) Federalist and Antifederalist Web Pages **[Below Level]**	___ Spanish/English Interactive Reader and Study Guide: Section 5
___ **Primary Source** (SE) *Federalist Paper* No. 10	___ Supreme Court Case Studies: *Schenck* v. *United States*
___ **Critical Thinking** (TE) *Federalist Paper* No. 51	
___ **Map** (SE) Ratification of the Constitution	
___ **Landmark Supreme Court Cases** (TE, SE) *Schenck* v. *United States* (1919)	
___ **We the People** (TE, SE) Individual Rights and the U.S. Constitution	
REVIEW & ASSESS	**RESOURCES**
___ **Close** (TE) Have students review the section by listing the events that led to the ratification of the Constitution.	___ Online Quiz Section 5 keyword: SGO ORI HP
___ **Section 5 Assessment** (SE)	___ PASS: Section 5 Quiz

Key: SE = Student Edition **TE** = Teacher's Edition **CRF** = Chapter Resource File

The Constitution

Lesson Plan

Section 1

Objectives Students will learn . . .	**Teacher Notes**
1. how the Constitution outlines six fundamental principles of U.S. government.	
2. how the Constitution limits the powers of government in order to protect individual rights.	
3. how the Constitution divides the powers of government among the legislative, executive, and judicial branches.	
4. how the Constitution includes checks and balances to prevent any one branch of government from overpowering the others.	
Key Terms Preteach the following terms: popular sovereignty, limited government, rule of law, separation of powers, checks and balances, veto, judicial review, unconstitutional, federalism	

PRETEACH	**RESOURCES**
___ **Before You Read . . .** (SE) Preview the Main Idea, Reading Focus, and Key Terms.	___ CRF: Vocabulary Builder: Section 1
___ **Academic Vocabulary** (SE) Review with students the high-use academic term in this section.	

DIRECT TEACH	**RESOURCES**
___ **Teach the Main Idea Activity** (TE) Students discuss the Reading Focus questions and identify the three branches of government and their constitutional powers.	___ Interactive Reader and Study Guide: Section 1
___ **Collaborative Learning** (TE) Constitutional Goals	___ Transparency: Quick Facts: Goals of the Constitution
___ **Differentiating Instruction: Special Needs Learners** (TE) Principles of the Constitution **[Below Level]**	
___ **Critical Thinking** (TE) Who are "the People"?	___ Transparency: Political Cartoon: Checks and Balances
___ **Differentiating Instruction: Advanced/Gifted and Talented** (TE) The Supreme Court **[Above Level]**	___ CRF: Biography: Patrick Henry
___ **Skills Focus** (TE) *Marbury* v. *Madison*	___ CRF: Primary Source: Albany Plan of Union
___ **Debating the Issue** (TE, SE) Constitution and Privacy	

REVIEW & ASSESS	**RESOURCES**
___ **Close** (TE) Guide students in a review of the ways the Constitution balances the powers of government.	___ Online Quiz Section 1 keyword: SGO CON HP
___ **Section 1 Assessment** (SE)	___ PASS: Section 1 Quiz

Key: SE = Student Edition **TE** = Teacher's Edition **CRF** = Chapter Resource File

The Constitution

Objectives Students will learn . . . 1. how Jefferson and Madison differed in their views on amending the Constitution. 2. why the Constitution can be called a document for all time. 3. the processes by which the Constitution can be amended. 4. what types of amendments have been added to the Constitution over the last 220 years. **Key Terms** Preteach the following terms: supermajority, repeal	**Teacher Notes**
PRETEACH	**RESOURCES**
___ **Before You Read . . .** (SE) Preview the Main Idea, Reading Focus, and Key Terms. ___ **Academic Vocabulary** (SE) Review with students the high-use academic term in this section.	___ CRF: Vocabulary Builder: Section 2 ___ Teacher One Stop™: Differentiated Instruction Modified Worksheets and Tests
DIRECT TEACH	**RESOURCES**
___ **Teach the Main Idea Activity** (TE) Students discuss the Reading Focus questions and create a flowchart showing the four ways in which proposed amendments can be ratified. ___ **Critical Thinking** (TE) A Constitution for Our Time ___ **Collaborative Learning** (TE) Amending the Constitution ___ **Differentiating Instruction: Struggling Readers** (TE) The Amendment Process **[Below Level]** ___ **Critical Thinking** (TE) Amendments That Failed	___ Interactive Reader and Study Guide: Section 2 ___ Transparency: Quick Facts: Amending the Constitution ___ Transparency: Quick Facts: Amendments to the Constitution ___ CRF: Primary Source: *Federalist Paper*, No. 49 ___ CRF: Political Cartoon: Amending the Constitution
REVIEW & ASSESS	**RESOURCES**
___ **Close** (TE) Guide students in a review of the amendment process and how it aligns with the views of Jefferson and Madison. ___ **Section 2 Assessment** (SE)	___ Online Quiz Section 2 keyword: SGO CON HP ___ PASS: Section 2 Quiz

Key: **SE** = Student Edition **TE** = Teacher's Edition **CRF** = Chapter Resource File

The Constitution

Lesson Plan

Section 3

Objectives Students will learn . . . 1. how the three branches of government have applied the Constitution. 2. how political parties, customs, and traditions have changed how the Constitution is applied. 3. what criticisms people have made of the Constitution. **Key Terms** Preteach the following terms: executive agreement, political party, cabinet, gridlock, electoral college	**Teacher Notes**

PRETEACH	**RESOURCES**
___ **Before You Read . . .** (SE) Preview the Main Idea, Reading Focus, and Key Terms. ___ **Academic Vocabulary** (SE) Review with students the high-use academic term in this section.	___ CRF: Vocabulary Builder: Section 3 ___ Teacher One Stop™: Differentiated Instruction Modified Worksheets and Tests

DIRECT TEACH	**RESOURCES**
___ **Teach the Main Idea Activity** (TE) Students discuss the Reading Focus questions and create an outline of the section. ___ **Critical Thinking** (TE) Executive Agreements ___ **Critical Thinking** (TE) Judicial Interpretation ___ **Collaborative Learning** (TE) Starting a Political Party ___ **Differentiating Instruction: Advanced/Gifted and Talented** (TE) Comparing Constitutions **[Above Level]** ___ **We the People** (TE, SE) A New Constitution and a New Government	___ Interactive Reader and Study Guide: Section 3 ___ Transparency: Quick Facts: The Enduring Constitution ___ Transparency: Political Cartoon: Gridlock in Government ___ CRF: Biography: Alexander Hamilton ___ CRF: Economics and Government: The Sixteenth Amendment

REVIEW & ASSESS	**RESOURCES**
___ **Close** (TE) Guide students in a review of the ways in which the three branches of government have developed over the past 220 years. ___ **Section 3 Assessment** (SE)	___ Online Quiz Section 3 keyword: SGO CON HP ___ PASS: Section 3 Quiz

Key: SE = Student Edition **TE** = Teacher's Edition **CRF** = Chapter Resource File

Federalism

Lesson Plan

Section 1

	Teacher Notes
Objectives Students will learn . . . 1. why the Framers chose a federal system of government. 2. the powers granted to the national government, those granted to state governments, and those shared by both national and state governments. 3. how the Constitution limits the powers of the state and national governments. 4. how the Constitution guides the relationships between the nation and the 50 states. **Key Terms** Preteach the following terms: expressed powers, implied powers, inherent powers, reserved powers, concurrent powers, full faith and credit clause	
PRETEACH	**RESOURCES**
____ **Before You Read . . .** (SE) Preview the Main Idea, Reading Focus, and Key Terms.	____ CRF: Vocabulary Builder: Section 1
DIRECT TEACH	**RESOURCES**
____ **Teach the Main Idea Activity** (TE) Students discuss the Reading Focus questions and identify the various powers granted to governments by the Constitution. ____ **Differentiating Instruction: Advanced/Gifted and Talented** (TE) Examining Federalism **[Above Level]** ____ **Critical Thinking** (TE) Powers of the Nation and of the States ____ **Collaborative Learning** (TE) Who Should Legislate? ____ **Differentiating Instruction: Struggling Readers** (TE) Comparing Powers **[Below Level]** ____ **Critical Thinking** (TE) Conflict between Governments	____ Interactive Reader and Study Guide: Section 1 ____ Transparency: Quick Facts: From Confederation to Federal System ____ Transparency: Quick Facts: Powers of the National Government ____ Transparency: Quick Facts: Powers of State Governments ____ Transparency: Quick Facts: Powers Shared by the Nation and the States
REVIEW & ASSESS	**RESOURCES**
____ **Close** (TE) Have students name national, state, and concurrent powers. ____ **Section 1 Assessment** (SE)	____ Online Quiz Section 1 keyword: SGO FED HP ____ PASS: Section 1 Quiz

Key: SE = Student Edition **TE** = Teacher's Edition **CRF** = Chapter Resource File

Federalism

Lesson Plan
Section 2

Objectives Students will learn . . . 1. what role the Supreme Court plays in the federal system. 2. how government power was divided in dual federalism. 3. what events caused the expansion of national power in the twentieth century. 4. what new federalism is and how it functions. **Key Terms** Preteach the following terms: dual federalism, doctrine of nullification, doctrine of secession, cooperative federalism, creative federalism, new federalism, devolution	**Teacher Notes**

PRETEACH	**RESOURCES**
____ **Before You Read . . .** (SE) Preview the Main Idea, Reading Focus, and Key Terms. ____ **Academic Vocabulary** (SE) Review with students the high-use academic terms in this section.	____ CRF: Vocabulary Builder: Section 2

DIRECT TEACH	**RESOURCES**
____ **Teach the Main Idea Activity** (TE) Students discuss the Reading Focus questions and create a time line illustrating the major periods of American federalism. ____ **Primary Source** (TE) *Federalist Paper* No. 10 ____ **Differentiating Instruction: English-Language Learners** (TE) Federalism Cartoons **[Below Level]** ____ **Collaborative Learning** (TE) Creative or New Federalism? ____ **Skills Focus** (TE) States in Rebellion ____ **Landmark Supreme Court Cases** (TE, SE) *McCulloch* v. *Maryland* (1819) ____ **Critical Thinking** (TE) Regulating Business ____ **Profiles in Government** (SE) Franklin D. Roosevelt ____ **Collaborative Learning** (TE) The New Deal ____ **Debating the Issue** (TE, SE) Federalism and Hurricane Katrina	____ Interactive Reader and Study Guide: Section 2 ____ Transparency: Political Cartoon: Monopoly Busting ____ CRF: Biographies: Lyndon B. Johnson, Ronald Reagan ____ CRF: Primary Source: Reagan on Government ____ Supreme Court Case Studies: *McCulloch* v. *Maryland, United States* v. *E.C. Knight Company*

REVIEW & ASSESS	**RESOURCES**
____ **Close** (TE) Discuss the ways in which the role of the national government has changed since its inception. ____ **Section 2 Assessment** (SE)	____ Online Quiz Section 2 keyword: SGO FED HP ____ PASS: Section 2 Quiz

Key: SE = Student Edition **TE** = Teacher's Edition **CRF** = Chapter Resource File

Federalism

Lesson Plan

Section 3

Objectives Students will learn . . . 1. what fiscal federalism is and how it works. 2. how the national government uses grants and mandates to influence state policies. 3. what issues influence American federalism today. **Key Terms** Preteach the following terms: fiscal federalism, grants-in-aid, categorical grants, block grants, federal mandates	**Teacher Notes**
PRETEACH	**RESOURCES**
___ **Before You Read . . .** (SE) Preview the Main Idea, Reading Focus, and Key Terms.	___ CRF: Vocabulary Builder: Section 3
DIRECT TEACH	**RESOURCES**
___ **Teach the Main Idea Activity** (TE) Students discuss the Reading Focus questions and create an outline of this section. ___ **Differentiating Instruction: Special Needs Learners** (TE) Federal Grants **[Below Level]** ___ **Critical Thinking** (TE) Unfunded Mandates ___ **We the People** (TE, SE) Laboratories of Democracy	___ Interactive Reader and Study Guide: Section 3 ___ Spanish/English Interactive Reader and Study Guide: Section 3 ___ Transparency: Political Cartoon: States Rights versus Congress ___ CRF: Economics and Government: Federal Mandate Funding ___ CRF: Political Cartoon: Hurricane Katrina
REVIEW & ASSESS	**RESOURCES**
___ **Close** (TE) Guide the class in a discussion of fiscal federalism and how it works. ___ **Section 3 Assessment** (SE)	___ Online Quiz Section 3 keyword: SGO FED HP ___ PASS: Section 3 Quiz

Key: SE = Student Edition **TE** = Teacher's Edition **CRF** = Chapter Resource File

Congress: The Legislative Branch

Lesson Plan

Section 1

Objectives Students will learn . . .	**Teacher Notes**
1. how Congress represents the people.	
2. why the structure of Congress is important.	
3. what the role of Congress is in the system of checks and balances.	
Key Terms Preteach the following terms: constituents, apportionment, appropriation, impeachment, oversight	

PRETEACH	**RESOURCES**
____ **Before You Read . . .** (SE) Preview the Main Idea, Reading Focus, and Key Terms.	____ CRF: Vocabulary Builder: Section 1
	____ Teacher One Stop™: Differentiated Instruction Modified Worksheets and Tests

DIRECT TEACH	**RESOURCES**
____ **Teach the Main Idea Activity** (TE) Students discuss the Reading Focus questions and review what they know of Congress in the system of checks and balances.	____ Interactive Reader and Study Guide: Section 1
____ **Differentiating Instruction: English-Language Learners** (TE) Creating a Crossword Puzzle **[Below Level]**	____ Spanish/English Interactive Reader and Study Guide: Section 1
____ **Interpreting Charts** (SE) Congressional Representation, Selected States, 2007	
____ **Critical Thinking** (TE) Legislative Branch Organizers	
____ **Collaborative Learning** (TE) Promoting Congress	

REVIEW & ASSESS	**RESOURCES**
____ **Close** (TE) Have students name the primary functions of Congress	____ Online Quiz Section 1 keyword: SGO CNG HP
____ **Section 1 Assessment** (SE)	
	____ PASS: Section 1 Quiz

Key: SE = Student Edition **TE** = Teacher's Edition **CRF** = Chapter Resource File

Congress: The Legislative Branch

Lesson Plan

Section 2

	Teacher Notes
Objectives Students will learn . . . 1. what types of powers Congress has. 2. the expressed, implied, and nonlegislative powers of Congress. 3. what limits exist on the powers of Congress. 4. how the powers of Congress have changed over time. **Key Terms** Preteach the following terms: necessary and proper clause, indirect tax, direct tax, deficit, commerce clause, subpoenas, writ of habeas corpus, bill of attainder, ex post facto laws	

PRETEACH	RESOURCES
___ **Before You Read . . .** (SE) Preview the Main Idea, Reading Focus, and Key Terms. ___ **Academic Vocabulary** (SE) Review with students the high-use academic terms in this section.	___ CRF: Vocabulary Builder: Section 2 ___ Teacher One Stop™: Differentiated Instruction Modified Worksheets and Tests

DIRECT TEACH	RESOURCES
___ **Teach the Main Idea Activity** (TE) Students discuss the Reading Focus questions and review what they know of the powers of Congress. ___ **Critical Thinking** (TE) Congressional Powers ___ **Differentiating Instruction: Struggling Readers** (TE) Reading Journals **[Below Level]** ___ **Collaborative Learning** (TE) Powers of Congress ___ **Landmark Supreme Court Cases** (TE, SE) *Gibbons v. Ogden* (1894) ___ **Differentiating Instruction: English-Language Learners** (TE) Understanding Vocabulary **[Below Level]** ___ **Skills Focus** (TE) Media Reports on Congress	___ Interactive Reader and Study Guide: Section 2 ___ Spanish/English Interactive Reader and Study Guide: Section 2 ___ CRF: Primary Source: War Powers Resolution, 1973 ___ Supreme Court Cases Studies: *Gibbons v. Ogden, Watkins v. United States*

REVIEW & ASSESS	RESOURCES
___ **Close** (TE) Have students discuss how Hamilton and Jefferson might view our modern Congress. ___ **Section 2 Assessment** (SE)	___ Online Quiz Section 2 keyword: SGO CNG HP ___ PASS: Section 2 Quiz

Key: SE = Student Edition **TE** = Teacher's Edition **CRF** = Chapter Resource File

Congress: The Legislative Branch

Lesson Plan

Section 3

Objectives Students will learn . . . 1. the key features of the House of Representatives and its members. 2. what challenges reapportionment and redistricting pose. 3. how the House leadership is organized. 4. what the role of committees is in the operation of the House of Representatives. **Key Terms** Preteach the following terms: reapportionment, gerrymandering, Speaker of the House, bills, floor leader, whips, party caucus, standing committees, select committees, joint committees	**Teacher Notes**

PRETEACH	**RESOURCES**
___ **Before You Read . . .** (SE) Preview the Main Idea, Reading Focus, and Key Terms. ___ **Academic Vocabulary** (SE) Review with students the high-use academic term in this section.	___ CRF: Vocabulary Builder: Section 3 ___ Teacher One Stop™: Differentiated Instruction Modified Worksheets and Tests

DIRECT TEACH	**RESOURCES**
___ **Teach the Main Idea Activity** (TE) Students discuss the Reading Focus questions and create an outline of this section. ___ **Critical Thinking** (TE) Job Opening: U.S. Representative ___ **Differentiating Instruction: Struggling Readers** (TE) Understanding Gerrymandering **[Below Level]** ___ **Skills Focus** (TE) U.S. Representatives ___ **Profiles in Government** (SE) Nancy Pelosi ___ **Collaborative Learning** (TE) Performing a Skit	___ Interactive Reader and Study Guide: Section 3 ___ Transparency: Political Cartoon: The Iron Duke, "Gerry Mander" ___ Transparency: Quick Facts: House of Representatives ___ CRF: Biography: War Jeannette Rankin ___ CRF: Primary Source: Nancy Pelosi Speech

REVIEW & ASSESS	**RESOURCES**
___ **Close** (TE) Have students discuss possible strengths and weaknesses in how the House of Representatives conducts its work. ___ **Section 3 Assessment** (SE)	___ Online Quiz Section 3 keyword: SGO CNG HP ___ PASS: Section 3 Quiz

Key: SE = Student Edition **TE** = Teacher's Edition **CRF** = Chapter Resource File

Congress: The Legislative Branch

Lesson Plan

Section 4

	Teacher Notes
Objectives Students will learn . . . 1. the major features of the Senate and its membership. 2. the Senate's leadership posts. 3. the role of committees in the Senate. 4. the distinctive rules and traditions of the Senate. **Key Terms** Preteach the following terms: president of the Senate, president pro tempore, Senate majority leader, seniority rule, filibuster, cloture	
PRETEACH	**RESOURCES**
____ **Before You Read . . .** (SE) Preview the Main Idea, Reading Focus, and Key Terms.	____ CRF: Vocabulary Builder: Section 4 ____ Teacher One Stop™: Differentiated Instruction Modified Worksheets and Tests
DIRECT TEACH	**RESOURCES**
____ **Teach the Main Idea Activity** (TE) Students discuss the Reading Focus questions and make a list of the characteristics of the Senate. ____ **Differentiating Instruction: English-Language Learners** (TE) Understanding Vocabulary **[Below Level]** ____ **Critical Thinking** (TE) Diversity in the Senate ____ **Collaborative Learning** (TE) Committee Posters ____ **Debating the Issue** (TE, SE) The Seniority System	____ Interactive Reader and Study Guide: Section 4 ____ Spanish/English Interactive Reader and Study Guide: Section 4 ____ Transparency: Quick Facts: Senate: Terms, Salary, Benefits, and Privileges ____ CRF: Biography: Robert Byrd
REVIEW & ASSESS	**RESOURCES**
____ **Close** (TE) Have students compile a list of at least 15 words that describe the Senate. ____ **Section 4 Assessment** (SE)	____ Online Quiz Section 4 keyword: SGO CNG HP ____ PASS: Section 4 Quiz

Key: SE = Student Edition **TE** = Teacher's Edition **CRF** = Chapter Resource File

Congress: The Legislative Branch

Lesson Plan

Section 5

Objectives Students will learn . . .	**Teacher Notes**
1. how bills are introduced in Congress.	
2. what happens to a bill in committee.	
3. what happens to a bill on the floor of the House and Senate.	
4. what a conference committee is and how it works.	
5. what actions a president can take on a bill.	
Key Terms Preteach the following terms: rider, joint resolution, concurrent resolutions, discharge petition, Committee of the Whole, quorum, roll-call vote, conference committee, pocket veto	
PRETEACH	**RESOURCES**
___ **Before You Read . . .** (SE) Preview the Main Idea, Reading Focus, and Key Terms.	___ CRF: Vocabulary Builder: Section 5
___ **Academic Vocabulary** (SE) Review with students the high-use academic term in this section.	___ Teacher One Stop™: Differentiated Instruction Modified Worksheets and Tests
DIRECT TEACH	**RESOURCES**
___ **Teach the Main Idea Activity** (TE) Students discuss the Reading Focus questions create a graphic organizer explaining how a bill becomes a law.	___ Interactive Reader and Study Guide: Section 5
___ **Critical Thinking** (TE) Drafting a Legislative Bill	___ Spanish/English Interactive Reader and Study Guide: Section 5
___ **Differentiating Instruction: Special Needs Learners** (TE) Explaining the Lawmaking Process **[Below Level]**	___ Transparency: Quick Facts: How a Bill Becomes a Law
___ **Critical Thinking** (TE) From Bill to Law	
___ **Critical Thinking** (TE) The Lawmaking Process	___ CRF: Biography: Robert Byrd
___ **Primary Sources** (SE) Pork-Barrel Spending	
___ **Skills Focus** (TE) Pork-Barrel Bills	
___ **We the People** (TE, SE) The Sources of Laws	
REVIEW & ASSESS	**RESOURCES**
___ **Close** (TE) Have students brainstorm and create a class list of words that can be used to describe the lawmaking process.	___ Online Quiz Section 5 keyword: SGO CNG HP
___ **Section 5 Assessment** (SE)	___ PASS: Section 5 Quiz

Key: SE = Student Edition **TE** = Teacher's Edition **CRF** = Chapter Resource File

The Presidency

Lesson Plan

Section 1

Objectives Students will learn . . .	**Teacher Notes**
1. the roles of the president.	
2. the formal characteristics of the president.	
3. the informal qualifications of the president.	
Key Terms Preteach the following terms: chief executive, commander in chief, foreign policy, diplomacy, chief of state, succession	
PRETEACH	**RESOURCES**
___ **Before You Read . . .** (SE) Preview the Main Idea, Reading Focus, and Key Terms.	___ CRF: Vocabulary Builder: Section 1
___ **Academic Vocabulary** (SE) Review with students the high-use academic term in this section.	___ Teacher One Stop™: Differentiated Instruction Modified Worksheets and Tests
DIRECT TEACH	**RESOURCES**
___ **Teach the Main Idea Activity** (TE) Students discuss the Reading Focus questions and create a chart that identifies the roles and qualifications of the president.	___ Interactive Reader and Study Guide: Section 1
___ **Critical Thinking** (TE) One or Two Executives?	___ Transparency: Quick Facts: The Electoral College
___ **Collaborative Learning** (TE) Only Two Terms?	
___ **Differentiating Instruction: English-Language Learners** (TE) The Electoral College **[Below Level]**	___ Transparency: Quick Facts: Presidential Succession
___ **Skills Focus** (TE) Electoral College Views	___ Transparency: Quick Facts: President and Vice President: Terms, Salary, and Benefits
___ **Differentiating Instruction: Special Needs Learners** (TE) Presidential Candidates **[At Level]**	
	___ CRF: Biography: George Washington
	___ CRF: Primary Source: Kennedy's Inaugural Address
REVIEW & ASSESS	**RESOURCES**
___ **Close** (TE) Have students review the qualifications and categories of duties of the president.	___ Online Quiz Section 1 keyword: SGO PRE HP
___ **Section 1 Assessment** (SE)	___ PASS: Section 1 Quiz

Key: SE = Student Edition **TE** = Teacher's Edition **CRF** = Chapter Resource File

The Presidency

Lesson Plan

Section 2

Objectives Students will learn . . . 1. the executive powers of the president. 2. the diplomatic and military powers of the president. 3. how the president exercises legislative and judicial powers. 4. the informal powers of the president. 5. how presidential powers are checked by the other branches. 6. how presidential powers have changed over the years. **Key Terms** Preteach the following terms: executive orders, executive privilege, diplomatic recognition, reprieve, pardon, amnesty, commute	**Teacher Notes**
PRETEACH	**RESOURCES**
___ **Before You Read . . .** (SE) Preview the Main Idea, Reading Focus, and Key Terms. ___ **Academic Vocabulary** (SE) Review with students the high-use academic term in this section.	___ CRF: Vocabulary Builder: Section 2
DIRECT TEACH	**RESOURCES**
___ **Teach the Main Idea Activity** (TE) Students discuss the Reading Focus questions and develop a bulleted list that identifies the different powers of the president. ___ **Differentiating Instruction: Struggling Readers** (TE) Presidential Powers **[Below Level]** ___ **Critical Thinking** (TE) Views on Watergate ___ **Differentiating Instruction: Special Needs Learners** (TE) The President's Diplomatic Powers **[Below Level]** ___ **Skills Focus** (TE) The War Powers Resolution ___ **Differentiating Instruction: Advanced/Gifted and Talented** (TE) Growth of Presidential Powers ___ **Debating the Issue** (TE, SE) The Power to Make War	___ Interactive Reader and Study Guide: Section 2 ___ Transparency: Political Cartoon: Declaring War ___ CRF: Biography: Abraham Lincoln ___ CRF: Primary Source: Washington's Farewell Address ___ Supreme Court Case Studies: *United States v. Nixon* and *Clinton v. City of New York*
REVIEW & ASSESS	**RESOURCES**
___ **Close** (TE) Have students compare the president's formal and informal powers. ___ **Section 2 Assessment** (SE)	___ Online Quiz Section 2 keyword: SGO PRE HP ___ PASS: Section 2 Quiz

Key: SE = Student Edition **TE** = Teacher's Edition **CRF** = Chapter Resource File

The Presidency

Lesson Plan

Section 3

Objectives Students will learn . . . 1. what the Executive Office of the President is and what its duties are. 2. how the role of the vice president has changed over time. 3. what the cabinet is and how it works with the president. **Key Terms** Preteach the following terms: administration, Executive Office of the President, White House Office, chief of staff, National Security Council, Council of Economic Advisers, Office of Management and Budget, executive departments	**Teacher Notes**

PRETEACH	RESOURCES
____ **Before You Read . . .** (SE) Preview the Main Idea, Reading Focus, and Key Terms. ____ **Academic Vocabulary** (SE) Review with students the high-use academic term in this section.	____ CRF: Vocabulary Builder: Section 3 ____ Teacher One Stop™: Differentiated Instruction Modified Worksheets and Tests

DIRECT TEACH	RESOURCES
____ **Teach the Main Idea Activity** (TE) Students discuss the Reading Focus questions and create a list of the duties and responsibilities of the people who work in the executive branch. ____ **Critical Thinking** (TE) The West Wing ____ **Differentiating Instruction: English-Language Learners** (TE) The President's Chief of Staff **[Below Level]** ____ **Critical Thinking** (TE) The President's Response ____ **Collaborative Learning** (TE) Cabinet Collage ____ **We the People** (TE, SE) Executive Power and the President	____ Interactive Reader and Study Guide: Section 3 ____ Spanish/English Interactive Reader and Study Guide: Section 3 ____ Transparency: Quick Facts: Selected White House Offices ____ CRF: Economics and Government: Presidents and Spending ____ Supreme Court Case Studies: Terrorism Cases

REVIEW & ASSESS	RESOURCES
____ **Close** (TE) Have students summarize the roles of the Executive Office of the President, the vice president, and the cabinet. ____ **Section 3 Assessment** (SE)	____ Online Quiz Section 3 keyword: SGO PRE HP ____ PASS: Section 3 Quiz

Key: SE = Student Edition **TE** = Teacher's Edition **CRF** = Chapter Resource File

The Executive Branch at Work

Lesson Plan
Section 1

Objectives Students will learn . . . 1. what the federal bureaucracy is. 2. what the civil service is and how it has changed over the years. **Key Terms** Preteach the following terms: bureaucracy, bureaucrats, civil service, spoils system	**Teacher Notes**

PRETEACH	RESOURCES
___ **Before You Read . . .** (SE) Preview the Main Idea, Reading Focus, and Key Terms. ___ **Academic Vocabulary** (SE) Review with students the high-use academic term in this section.	___ CRF: Vocabulary Builder: Section 1 ___ Teacher One Stop™: Differentiated Instruction Modified Worksheets and Tests

DIRECT TEACH	RESOURCES
___ **Teach the Main Idea Activity** (TE) Students discuss the Reading Focus questions and identify and rank the ways in which the federal bureaucracy has changed over the years. ___ **Interpreting Charts** (SE) The Executive Branch ___ **Differentiating Instruction: English-Language Learners** (TE) Federal Bureaucracy Collage **[Below Level]** ___ **Primary Source** (SE) The Spoils System ___ **Critical Thinking** (TE) Civil Service Time Line	___ Interactive Reader and Study Guide: Section 1 ___ Spanish/English Interactive Reader and Study Guide: Section 1 ___ Transparency: Political Cartoon: The Spoils System

REVIEW & ASSESS	RESOURCES
___ **Close** (TE) Guide students in a discussion of how the national government hires people to carry out its work. ___ **Section 1 Assessment** (SE)	___ Online Quiz Section 1 keyword: SGO EXE HP ___ PASS: Section 1 Quiz

Key: SE = Student Edition **TE** = Teacher's Edition **CRF** = Chapter Resource File

The Executive Branch at Work | Lesson Plan

	Teacher Notes
Objectives Students will learn . . . 1. the purpose of the executive department. 2. what the primary functions of the executive departments are today. 3. what independent agencies are and how they work. 4. what the issues are regarding power and accountability in the federal bureaucracy. **Key Terms** Preteach the following terms: independent agencies, independent executive agencies, independent regulatory commissions, bipartisan, government corporations	

PRETEACH	**RESOURCES**
___ **Before You Read . . .** (SE) Preview the Main Idea, Reading Focus, and Key Terms. ___ **Academic Vocabulary** (SE) Review with students the high-use academic terms in this section.	___ CRF: Vocabulary Builder: Section 2

DIRECT TEACH	**RESOURCES**
___ **Teach the Main Idea Activity** (TE) Students discuss the Reading Focus questions and identify the executive departments and independent agencies. ___ **Collaborative Learning** (TE) Creating an Executive Department ___ **Interpreting Charts** (SE) The Executive Departments ___ **Differentiating Instruction: English-Language Learners** (TE) Understanding Executive Departments ___ **Critical Thinking** (TE) Executive Departments ___ **Skills Focus** (TE) Federal Agency Presentations ___ **Skills Focus** (TE) Government Corporations ___ **Landmark Supreme Court Cases** (TE, SE) *Schechter Poultry Corporation* v. *United States* (1935) ___ **Debating the Issue** (TE, SE) The Size of the Federal Bureaucracy	___ Interactive Reader and Study Guide: Section 2 ___ Transparency: Political Cartoon: Streamlining the Bureaucracy ___ CRF: Biographies: Madeleine Albright, Colin Powell ___ CRF: Primary Source: Bush on Homeland Security ___ Supreme Court Case Studies: New Deal Cases, *Northern Securities Co.* v. *United States*

REVIEW & ASSESS	**RESOURCES**
___ **Close** (TE) Have students list the executive departments and executive agencies. ___ **Section 2 Assessment** (SE)	___ Online Quiz Section 2 keyword: SGO EXE HP ___ PASS: Section 2 Quiz

Key: SE = Student Edition **TE** = Teacher's Edition **CRF** = Chapter Resource File

The Executive Branch at Work

Lesson Plan
Section 3

Objectives Students will learn . . . 1. how the federal government pays for its operations. 2. the two types of government spending. 3. how the federal budget process works. 4. how fiscal and monetary policy affect the nation's economy. **Key Terms** Preteach the following terms: income tax, progressive tax, payroll tax, regressive tax, proportional tax, bond, federal debt, mandatory spending, discretionary spending, fiscal policy, monetary policy	**Teacher Notes**

PRETEACH	RESOURCES
____ **Before You Read . . .** (SE) Preview the Main Idea, Reading Focus, and Key Terms. ____ **Academic Vocabulary** (SE) Review with students the high-use academic term in this section.	____ CRF: Vocabulary Builder: Section 3

DIRECT TEACH	RESOURCES
____ **Teach the Main Idea Activity** (TE) Students discuss the Reading Focus questions and brainstorm ideas about how the government raises and spends money. ____ **Differentiating Instruction: Struggling Readers** (TE) Creating a Quiz **[Below Level]** ____ **Collaborative Learning** (TE) The Effect of Taxes ____ **Critical Thinking** (TE) Government Financing ____ **Differentiating Instruction: English-Language Learners** (TE) Federal Budget Process **[Below Level]** ____ **Critical Thinking** (TE) Budget Process Jingle ____ **Interpreting Charts** (SE) Fiscal Policy ____ **Critical Thinking** (TE) Tax Cuts v. Increase Spending ____ **Profiles in Government** (SE) Benjamin Bernanke ____ **We the People** (TE, SE) The Federal Bureaucracy	____ Interactive Reader and Study Guide: Section 3 ____ Transparency: Quick Facts: Fiscal Policy and the Economy ____ Transparency: Political Cartoon: Federal Debt ____ CRF: Primary Source: Two Views on the Budget ____ CRF: Political Cartoon: Taxes ____ CRF: Economics and Government: The Social Security Challenge

REVIEW & ASSESS	RESOURCES
____ **Close** (TE) Have students discuss the strengths and weaknesses of the federal government's finance system. ____ **Section 3 Assessment** (SE)	____ Online Quiz Section 3 keyword: SGO EXE HP ____ PASS: Section 3 Quiz

Key: SE = Student Edition **TE** = Teacher's Edition **CRF** = Chapter Resource File

The Federal Courts and the Judicial Branch

Lesson Plan

Section 1

Objectives Students will learn . . . 1. how jurisdiction is determined in the American court system. 2. how the federal court system is structured. 3. how federal judges are appointed. 4. what the role of the judicial branch is in the system of checks and balances. **Key Terms** Preteach the following terms: jurisdiction, exclusive jurisdiction, concurrent jurisdiction, plaintiff, defendant, original jurisdiction, appellate jurisdiction, judicial restraint, judicial activism, precedent, senatorial courtesy	**Teacher Notes**

PRETEACH	**RESOURCES**
___ **Before You Read . . .** (SE) Preview the Main Idea, Reading Focus, and Key Terms. ___ **Academic Vocabulary** (SE) Review with students the high-use academic term in this section.	___ CRF: Vocabulary Builder: Section 1 ___ Teacher One Stop™: Differentiated Instruction Modified Worksheets and Tests

DIRECT TEACH	**RESOURCES**
___ **Teach the Main Idea Activity** (TE) Students discuss the Reading Focus questions and write definitions for key terms in the section. ___ **Differentiating Instruction: Special Needs Learners** (TE) Comparing and Contrasting State and Federal Jurisdiction [Below Level] ___ **Interpreting Charts** (SE) The Federal Court System ___ **Differentiating Instruction: English-Language Learners** (TE) Civil and Criminal Cases [At Level] ___ **Skills Focus** (TE) Senate Confirmations ___ **Collaborative Learning** (TE) Senatorial Courtesy ___ **Debating the Issue** (TE, SE) Judicial Activism or Judicial Restraint?	___ Interactive Reader and Study Guide: Section 1 ___ Transparency: Quick Facts: Exclusive Jurisdiction of Federal Courts ___ Transparency: Quick Facts: Federal Judiciary ___ CRF: Primary Sources: Blackstone's *Commentaries* and *Federalist Paper* No. 78

REVIEW & ASSESS	**RESOURCES**
___ **Close** (TE) Discuss with students how the federal court system works. ___ **Section 1 Assessment** (SE)	___ Online Quiz Section 1 keyword: SGO JUD HP ___ PASS: Section 1 Quiz

Key: SE = Student Edition **TE** = Teacher's Edition **CRF** = Chapter Resource File

The Federal Courts and the Judicial Branch   Lesson Plan

Section 2

Objectives Students will learn . . .	**Teacher Notes**
1. the roles, jurisdiction, and officers of the federal district courts.	
2. the roles, jurisdiction, and procedures of the federal courts of appeals.	
3. how federal judges are appointed.	
4. the functions of some of the other federal courts.	
Key Terms Preteach the following terms: grand juries, bankruptcy, magistrate judges, misdemeanor, public defenders, marshals, appellant, briefs, sovereign immunity, courts-martial	

PRETEACH	**RESOURCES**
___ **Before You Read . . .** (SE) Preview the Main Idea, Reading Focus, and Key Terms.	___ CRF: Vocabulary Builder: Section 2
___ **Academic Vocabulary** (SE) Review with students the high-use academic term in this section.	___ Teacher One Stop™: Differentiated Instruction Modified Worksheets and Tests

DIRECT TEACH	**RESOURCES**
___ **Teach the Main Idea Activity** (TE) Students discuss the Reading Focus questions and identify the three types of lower federal courts and their functions.	___ Interactive Reader and Study Guide: Section 2
___ **Interpreting Charts** (SE) Federal Courts Caseload	___ Spanish/English Interactive Reader and Study Guide: Section 2
___ **Map** (SE) U.S. Federal Court Circuits and Districts	
___ **Differentiating Instruction: Struggling Readers** (TE) Federal Court Circuits and Districts **[Below Level]**	___ CRF: Biography: Janet Reno
___ **Critical Thinking** (TE) Federal Court Positions	___ Supreme Court Case Studies: *Alden* v. *Maine*
___ **Interpreting Charts** (SE) U.S. Courts of Appeals Caseload	
___ **Critical Thinking** (TE) The Federal Court System	
___ **Skills Focus** (TE) Judges and Juries	

REVIEW & ASSESS	**RESOURCES**
___ **Close** (TE) Have students review the different types of federal courts.	___ Online Quiz Section 2 keyword: SGO JUD HP
___ **Section 2 Assessment** (SE)	___ PASS: Section 2 Quiz

Key: SE = Student Edition **TE** = Teacher's Edition **CRF** = Chapter Resource File

The Federal Courts and the Judicial Branch   Lesson Plan

Section 3

Objectives Students will learn . . . 1. some of the highlights of Supreme Court history. 2. how Supreme Court justices are chosen. 3. the typical procedures of the Supreme Court. **Key Terms** Preteach the following terms: writ of certiorari, docket, majority opinion, concurring opinions, dissenting opinions	**Teacher Notes**

PRETEACH	**RESOURCES**
____ **Before You Read . . .** (SE) Preview the Main Idea, Reading Focus, and Key Terms. ____ **Academic Vocabulary** (SE) Review with students the high-use academic term in this section.	____ CRF: Vocabulary Builder: Section 3

DIRECT TEACH	**RESOURCES**
____ **Teach the Main Idea Activity** (TE) Students discuss the Reading Focus questions and create an outline of the section. ____ **Differentiating Instruction: English-Language Learners** (TE) Supreme Court Milestones **[Below Level]** ____ **Critical Thinking** (TE) The *Dred Scott* Decision ____ **Critical Thinking** (TE) *Civil Rights Cases* ____ **Landmark Supreme Court Cases** (SE) *Plessy* v. *Ferguson* (1896) ____ **Collaborative Learning** (TE) Separate but Equal? ____ **Skills Focus** (TE) Supreme Court Nominees ____ **Skills Focus** (TE) Supreme Court Rulings ____ **Critical Thinking** (TE) Dissenting Opinions ____ **We the People** (TE, SE) The Supreme Court and the System of Checks and Balances	____ Interactive Reader and Study Guide: Section 3 ____ Transparency: Political Cartoon: Confirmation Hearings ____ Transparency: Quick Facts: How Supreme Court Decisions Get Made ____ CRF: Biography: Oliver Wendall Holmes ____ CRF: Economics and Government: Monopolies and the Supreme Court ____ Supreme Court Case Studies: *Worcester* v. *Georgia* and *Lochner* v. *New York*

REVIEW & ASSESS	**RESOURCES**
____ **Close** (TE) Lead a class discussion of the importance of the Supreme Court as the final word on questions of federal law and the Constitution. ____ **Section 3 Assessment** (SE)	____ Online Quiz Section 3 keyword: SGO JUD HP ____ PASS: Section 3 Quiz

Key: SE = Student Edition **TE** = Teacher's Edition **CRF** = Chapter Resource File

The Political Process

Lesson Plan
Section 1

	Teacher Notes
Objectives Students will learn . . . 1. what public opinion is. 2. how public opinion is formed. 3. how the media affects public opinion. 4. how public opinion is measured. **Key Terms** Preteach the following terms: public opinion, public policy, political socialization, mass media, propaganda, poll, sample, sampling error, bias, objectivity, exit poll	

PRETEACH	**RESOURCES**
___ **Before You Read . . .** (SE) Preview the Main Idea, Reading Focus, and Key Terms. ___ **Academic Vocabulary** (SE) Review with students the high-use academic terms in this section.	___ CRF: Vocabulary Builder: Section 1 ___ Teacher One Stop™: Differentiated Instruction Modified Worksheets and Tests

DIRECT TEACH	**RESOURCES**
___ **Teach the Main Idea Activity** (TE) Students discuss the Reading Focus questions and write definitions for the key terms in the section. ___ **Interpreting Charts** (SE) Public Opinion over the Vietnam War ___ **Critical Thinking** (TE) Many Publics ___ **Differentiating Instruction: Special Needs Learners** (TE) Socialization and the Media **[Below Level]** ___ **Interpreting Charts (SE)** Source of News in Daily Life ___ **Skills Focus** (TE) Media Bias ___ **Interpreting Charts** (SE) Scientific Polling ___ **Collaborative Learning** (TE) Conducting Polls	___ Interactive Reader and Study Guide: Section 1 ___ Spanish/English Interactive Reader and Study Guide: Section 1 ___ CRF: Political Cartoon: Public Opinion Polls ___ CRF: Biography: George Gallup

REVIEW & ASSESS	**RESOURCES**
___ **Close** (TE) Guide students in a discussion of the part that public opinion plays in American political life. ___ **Section 1 Assessment** (SE)	___ Online Quiz Section 1 keyword: SGO POL HP ___ PASS: Section 1 Quiz

Key: **SE** = Student Edition **TE** = Teacher's Edition **CRF** = Chapter Resource File

The Political Process

Lesson Plan

Section 2

Objectives Students will learn . . . 1. what interest groups are and what role they play in the political process. 2. what different types of interest groups exist. 3. how interest groups work. 4. how interest groups serve the public good. **Key Terms** Preteach the following terms: interest group, political action committee, trade association, labor unions, endorse, lobbying, grass roots	**Teacher Notes**
PRETEACH	**RESOURCES**
___ **Before You Read . . .** (SE) Preview the Main Idea, Reading Focus, and Key Terms.	___ CRF: Vocabulary Builder: Section 2 ___ Teacher One Stop™: Differentiated Instruction Modified Worksheets and Tests
DIRECT TEACH	**RESOURCES**
___ **Teach the Main Idea Activity** (TE) Students discuss the Reading Focus questions and identify the six different types of interest groups and examples of each. ___ **Skills Focus** (TE) Interest Groups ___ **Skills Focus** (TE) Interest Group Tactics ___ **Primary Source** (TE) *Democracy in America* ___ **Differentiating Instruction: English-Language Learners** (TE) Types of Interest Groups **[Below Level]** ___ **Profiles in Government** (SE) Fannie Lou Hamer ___ **Critical Thinking** (TE) Assessing Interest Groups	___ Interactive Reader and Study Guide: Section 2 ___ Transparency: Political Cartoon: Interest Groups and Their Impact ___ CRF: Economics and Government: PACS and Election Politics ___ CRF: Biography: Ethel Percy Andrus ___ Supreme Court Case Studies: *In Re Debs*
REVIEW & ASSESS	**RESOURCES**
___ **Close** (TE) Guide students in a discussion of interest groups and the role they play in the political process. ___ **Section 2 Assessment** (SE)	___ Online Quiz Section 2 keyword: SGO POL HP ___ PASS: Section 2 Quiz

Key: SE = Student Edition **TE** = Teacher's Edition **CRF** = Chapter Resource File

The Political Process

Lesson Plan

Section 3

Objectives Students will learn . . .	Teacher Notes
1. what political parties are and what role they play in the political process.	
2. how the American two-party political system works.	
3. how political parties are organized.	
4. how political parties serve the public good.	
Key Terms Preteach the following terms: political party, political spectrum, nomination process, electorate, one-party system, two-party system, multiparty system, third party, independent candidate, precinct, ward	

PRETEACH	RESOURCES
___ **Before You Read . . .** (SE) Preview the Main Idea, Reading Focus, and Key Terms.	___ CRF: Vocabulary Builder: Section 3
___ **Academic Vocabulary** (SE) Review with students the high-use academic terms in this section.	

DIRECT TEACH	RESOURCES
___ **Teach the Main Idea Activity** (TE) Students discuss the Reading Focus questions and create an outline of this section.	___ Interactive Reader and Study Guide: Section 3
___ **Critical Thinking** (TE) The Political Spectrum	___ Spanish/English Interactive Reader and Study Guide: Section 3
___ **Differentiating Instruction: Advanced/Gifted and Talented** (TE) Two-Party Systems around the World **[Above Level]**	___ Transparency: Political Cartoon: Interest Groups and Their Impact
___ **Interpreting Charts** (SE) American Political Parties	
___ **Collaborative Learning** (TE) Third Party Politics	
___ **Differentiating Instruction: Struggling Readers** (TE) Local Party Organization **[Below Level]**	___ CRF: Primary Source: Thomas Jefferson on Partisanship
___ **Debating the Issue** (TE, SE) Voting for a Third-Party Candidate	

REVIEW & ASSESS	RESOURCES
___ **Close** (TE) Have students review the three main party systems.	___ Online Quiz Section 3 keyword: SGO POL HP
___ **Section 3 Assessment** (SE)	___ PASS: Section 3 Quiz

Key: SE = Student Edition **TE** = Teacher's Edition **CRF** = Chapter Resource File

The Political Process

Objectives Students will learn . . . 1. how a political campaign is organized and financed. 2. how candidates are chosen for an election. 3. what factors influence voting and voter behavior. 4. what the difference is between a general and a special election. 5. how political campaigns serve the public good **Key Terms** Preteach the following terms: hard money, soft money, write-in candidates, caucus, direct primary, closed primary, plurality, absentee ballot	**Teacher Notes**
PRETEACH	**RESOURCES**
____ **Before You Read . . .** (SE) Preview the Main Idea, Reading Focus, and Key Terms. ____ **Academic Vocabulary** (SE) Review with students the high-use academic terms in this section.	____ CRF: Vocabulary Builder: Section 4 ____ Teacher One Stop™: Differentiated Instruction Modified Worksheets and Tests
DIRECT TEACH	**RESOURCES**
____ **Teach the Main Idea Activity** (TE) Students discuss the Reading Focus questions and create a flowchart showing the steps of the electoral process. ____ **Critical Thinking** (TE) Campaigning or Serving ____ **Collaborative Learning** (TE) Caucuses and Primaries ____ **Differentiating Instruction: English Language-Learners** (TE) Improving Voter Turnout **[At Level]** ____ **Primary Sources** (SE) Politics and the Net ____ **Critical Thinking** (TE) Special Elections ____ **Landmark Supreme Court Cases** (SE) *Buckley* v. *Valeo* (1976) ____ **We the People** (TE, SE) The Role of Political Parties in the Constitutional System	____ Interactive Reader and Study Guide: Section 4 ____ CRF: Primary Source: 2004 Democratic and Republican Party Platforms ____ Supreme Court Case Studies: *Buckley* v. *Valeo* ____ Transparency: Political Cartoon: Feeding from the Trough
REVIEW & ASSESS	**RESOURCES**
____ **Close** (TE) Have students summarize the U.S. electoral process. ____ **Section 4 Assessment** (SE)	____ Online Quiz Section 4 keyword: SGO POL HP ____ PASS: Section 4 Quiz

Key: SE = Student Edition **TE** = Teacher's Edition **CRF** = Chapter Resource File

Civil Liberties

Lesson Plan
Section 1

Objectives Students will learn . . . 1. what the Bill of Rights is and what it protects. 2. what the limitations are on civil rights and civil liberties. 3. how the Fourteenth Amendment helps to protect civil liberties. **Key Terms** Preteach the following terms: public opinion, civil liberties, civil rights, due process, incorporation doctrine	**Teacher Notes**
PRETEACH	**RESOURCES**
___ **Before You Read . . .** (SE) Preview the Main Idea, Reading Focus, and Key Terms.	___ CRF: Vocabulary Builder: Section 1 ___ Teacher One Stop™: Differentiated Instruction Modified Worksheets and Tests
DIRECT TEACH	**RESOURCES**
___ **Teach the Main Idea Activity** (TE) Students discuss the Reading Focus questions and list the constitutional rights granted to Americans in the Bill of Rights. ___ **Profiles in Government** (SE) George Mason ___ **Differentiating Instruction: English-Language Learners** (TE) Understanding Concepts **[Below Level]** ___ **Primary Source** (TE) *Antifederalist Paper* No. 84 ___ **Interpreting Charts** (SE) Bill of Rights ___ **Skills Focus** (TE) Adopting the Bill of Rights ___ **Critical Thinking** (TE) Conflicting Rights	___ Interactive Reader and Study Guide: Section 1 ___ Transparency: Quick Facts: Bill of Rights ___ Transparency: Quick Facts: Process of Incorporation ___ CRF: Political Cartoon: Freedom of the Press ___ Supreme Court Case Studies: *Muller* v. *Oregon* and *Near* v. *Minnesota*
REVIEW & ASSESS	**RESOURCES**
___ **Close** (TE) Guide students in a discussion of how a nation benefits from a written bill of rights. ___ **Section 1 Assessment** (SE)	___ Online Quiz Section 1 keyword: SGO CLB HP ___ PASS: Section 1 Quiz

Key: SE = Student Edition **TE** = Teacher's Edition **CRF** = Chapter Resource File

Civil Liberties

Lesson Plan

Objectives Students will learn . . .	**Teacher Notes**
1. how the First Amendment guarantees religious freedom.	
2. what guarantees and limits exist on the freedoms of speech and of the press.	
3. what guarantees and limits exist on the freedoms of assembly and petition.	
Key Terms Preteach the following terms: establishment clause, free exercise clause, slander, libel, treason, sedition, prior restraint, symbolic speech, freedom of association	
PRETEACH	**RESOURCES**
____ **Before You Read . . .** (SE) Preview the Main Idea, Reading Focus, and Key Terms.	____ CRF: Vocabulary Builder: Section 2
DIRECT TEACH	**RESOURCES**
____ **Teach the Main Idea Activity** (TE) Students discuss the Reading Focus questions and identify and discuss the five freedoms granted by the First Amendment.	____ Interactive Reader and Study Guide: Section 2
____ **Skills Focus** (TE) First Amendment Speeches	____ Spanish/English Interactive Reader and Study Guide: Section 2
____ **Collaborative Learning** (TE) Religious Displays and the Constitution	____ Transparency: Political Cartoon: Separation of Church and State
____ **Critical Thinking** (TE) Religious Freedom in the United States	
____ **Primary Sources** (SE) The Fundamental Rights	
____ **Differentiating Instruction: Special Needs Learners** (TE) Understanding the Text **[Below Level]**	____ CRF: Primary Source: Brandeis on Freedom of Speech
____ **Profiles in Government** (SE) Louis Brandies	____ Supreme Court Case Studies: Freedom of Speech Cases
____ **Skills Focus** (TE) First Amendment and Libel	
____ **Collaborative Learning** (TE) Supreme Court and Free Speech	
____ **Critical Thinking** (TE) Speech and Press Outline	
____ **Debating the Issue** (TE, SE) Prayer in Public Schools	
REVIEW & ASSESS	**RESOURCES**
____ **Close** (TE) Have students discuss the importance of the First Amendment in the nation's democratic system.	____ Online Quiz Section 2 keyword: SGO CLB HP
____ **Section 2 Assessment** (SE)	____ PASS: Section 2 Quiz

Key: SE = Student Edition **TE** = Teacher's Edition **CRF** = Chapter Resource File

Civil Liberties

Lesson Plan
Section 3

Objectives Students will learn . . .	**Teacher Notes**
1. the purposes of and limits to the right to keep and bear arms.	
2. how the Bill of Rights guarantees the security of home and person.	
3. how the right to privacy has developed.	
4. how and why the Constitution guarantees due process of law.	
Key Terms Preteach the following terms: probable cause, search warrant, exclusionary rule, police power, procedural due process, substantive due process	

PRETEACH	**RESOURCES**
___ **Before You Read . . .** (SE) Preview the Main Idea, Reading Focus, and Key Terms. ___ **Academic Vocabulary** (SE) Review with students the high-use academic term in this section.	___ CRF: Vocabulary Builder: Section 3

DIRECT TEACH	**RESOURCES**
___ **Teach the Main Idea Activity** (TE) Students discuss the Reading Focus questions and identify the provisions of the Second, Third, Fourth, and Fifth Amendments. ___ **Differentiating Instruction: Struggling Readers** (TE) Discussing the Second Amendment **[Below Level]** ___ **Collaborative Learning** (TE) Revising the Fourth Amendment ___ **Primary Sources** (SE) Government Surveillance ___ **Skills Focus** (TE) Fourth Amendment Cartoons ___ **Differentiating Instruction: English-Language Learners** (TE) Creating a Policy Proposal **[Below Level]** ___ **Map** (SE) Surveillance and the Right to Privacy ___ **Skills Focus** (TE) Debating Privacy Rights	___ Interactive Reader and Study Guide: Section 3 ___ Transparency: Political Cartoon: Government Surveillance ___ Transparency: Quick Facts: Due Process ___ CRF: Primary Source: Truman on Human Liberty ___ Supreme Court Case Studies: *Yick Wo* v. *Hopkins*, *Weeks* v. *United States*, and *Mapp* v. *Ohio*

REVIEW & ASSESS	**RESOURCES**
___ **Close** (TE) Have students list Supreme Court decisions that relate to the Second, Third and Fourth Amendments. ___ **Section 3 Assessment** (SE)	___ Online Quiz Section 3 keyword: SGO CLB HP ___ PASS: Section 3 Quiz

Key: SE = Student Edition **TE** = Teacher's Edition **CRF** = Chapter Resource File

Civil Liberties

Lesson Plan

Section 4

Objectives Students will learn . . .	**Teacher Notes**
1. how the U.S. justice system addresses both civil and criminal law.	
2. how the Constitution guarantees the rights of those accused of a crime.	
3. the major constitutional guarantees for assuring fair trials.	
4. how the Constitution addresses the punishment of persons convicted of crimes.	
Key Terms Preteach the following terms: civil law, criminal law, indictment, bail, capital punishment, Miranda warnings, bench trial, double jeopardy	
PRETEACH	**RESOURCES**
___ **Before You Read . . .** (SE) Preview the Main Idea, Reading Focus, and Key Terms.	___ CRF: Vocabulary Builder: Section 4
___ **Academic Vocabulary** (SE) Review with students the high-use academic terms in this section.	
DIRECT TEACH	**RESOURCES**
___ **Teach the Main Idea Activity** (TE) Students discuss the Reading Focus questions and identify the rights of those accused of a crime.	___ Interactive Reader and Study Guide: Section 4
___ **Differentiating Instruction: English-Language Learners** (TE) Understanding Vocabulary [Below Level]	___ Transparency: Quick Facts: Protections for the Accused
___ **Critical Thinking** (TE) Rights of the Accused	___ CRF: Biographies: Earl Warren and Clarence Gideon
___ **Skills Focus** (TE) Miranda Rights	
___ **Landmark Supreme Court Cases** (TE, SE) *Miranda* v. *Arizona*	___ Supreme Court Case Studies: *Powell* v. *State of Alabama*, *Miranda* v. *Arizona*, and Death Penalty Cases
___ **Primary Sources** (SE) The Right to an Attorney	
___ **Critical Thinking** (TE) Supreme Court Decisions	
___ **We the People** (TE, SE) Fundamental Rights and the Doctrine of Incorporation	
REVIEW & ASSESS	**RESOURCES**
___ **Close** (TE) Have students list the protections that the Constitution provides to people accused of a crime.	___ Online Quiz Section 4 keyword: SGO CLB HP
___ **Section 4 Assessment** (SE)	___ PASS: Section 4 Quiz

Key: SE = Student Edition **TE** = Teacher's Edition **CRF** = Chapter Resource File

Civil Rights

Lesson Plan

Section 1

Objectives Students will learn . . . 1. what civil rights are and how civil rights in the United States have changed over time. 2. how a pattern of discrimination has affected the civil rights of some groups in U.S. history.. **Key Terms** Preteach the following terms: prejudice, racism, reservation, Japanese American internment	**Teacher Notes**
PRETEACH	**RESOURCES**
___ **Before You Read . . .** (SE) Preview the Main Idea, Reading Focus, and Key Terms. ___ **Academic Vocabulary** (SE) Review with students the high-use academic term in this section.	___ CRF: Vocabulary Builder: Section 1 ___ Teacher One Stop™: Differentiated Instruction Modified Worksheets and Tests
DIRECT TEACH	**RESOURCES**
___ **Teach the Main Idea Activity** (TE) Students discuss the Reading Focus questions and identify forms of discrimination and the groups that have been discriminated against. ___ **Critical Thinking** (TE) Civil Rights of Teenagers ___ **Skills Focus** (TE) Native American Citizenship ___ **Differentiating Instruction: Struggling Readers** (TE) Americanization **[Below Level]**	___ Interactive Reader and Study Guide: Section 1 ___ Spanish/English Interactive Reader and Study Guide: Section 1 ___ Transparency: Quick Facts: Civil Rights ___ CRF: Economics and Government: The Gender Wage Gap ___ Supreme Court Case Studies: *Dred Scott* v. *Sandford*
REVIEW & ASSESS	**RESOURCES**
___ **Close** (TE) Guide students in a discussion of the ways in which women and minorities have been discriminated against in the United States. ___ **Section 1 Assessment** (SE)	___ Online Quiz Section 1 keyword: SGO CRT HP ___ PASS: Section 1 Quiz

Key: SE = Student Edition **TE** = Teacher's Edition **CRF** = Chapter Resource File

Civil Rights

Lesson Plan

Section 2

Objectives Students will learn . . .	**Teacher Notes**
1. what is meant by equal protection of the law.	
2. what civil rights laws were passed after the Civil War and why they failed to end segregation.	
3. how women fought for and won voting rights.	
4. what events began to roll back racial and ethnic segregation in the United States.	
Key Terms Preteach the following terms: equal protection clause, suspect classification, segregation, Jim Crow laws, separate-but-equal doctrine, suffrage, Seneca Falls Convention, de jure segregation, desegregation, de facto segregation	

PRETEACH	**RESOURCES**
___ **Before You Read . . .** (SE) Preview the Main Idea, Reading Focus, and Key Terms.	___ CRF: Vocabulary Builder: Section 2
___ **Academic Vocabulary** (SE) Review with students the high-use academic term in this section.	

DIRECT TEACH	**RESOURCES**
___ **Teach the Main Idea Activity** (TE) Students discuss the Reading Focus questions and create a time line depicting African Americans' struggle for civil rights.	___ Interactive Reader and Study Guide: Section 2
___ **Critical Thinking** (TE) Equal Protection	___ CRF: Biography: Women's Suffrage Leaders
___ **Differentiating Instruction: Advanced/Gifted and Talented** (TE) The Rights of Enemy Combatants	___ CRF: Primary Source: Equal Rights for Women
___ **Critical Thinking** (TE) Reconstructing History	
___ **Critical Thinking** (TE) Jim Crow Laws	___ Supreme Court Case Studies: Civil Rights Cases, *United States* v. *Virginia*
___ **Primary Source** (TE) Equal Rights Amendment	
___ **Critical Thinking** (TE) Fifteenth and Nineteenth Amendments	
___ **Profiles in Government** (SE) Thurgood Marshall	
___ **Skills Focus** (TE) The Legacy of *Brown*	

REVIEW & ASSESS	**RESOURCES**
___ **Close** (TE) Have students discuss the struggle of African Americans and women to win equal treatment.	___ Online Quiz Section 2 keyword: SGO CRT HP
___ **Section 2 Assessment** (SE)	___ PASS: Section 2 Quiz

Key: SE = Student Edition **TE** = Teacher's Edition **CRF** = Chapter Resource File

Civil Rights

Lesson Plan

Section 3

Objectives Students will learn . . . 1. what the civil rights movement was and what effects it had on American society. 2. what new federal laws were passed in response to the civil rights movement. 3. how civil rights were extended to women, minorities, and people with disabilities. 4. how affirmative action polices were a part of the civil rights movement. **Key Terms** Preteach the following terms: civil rights movement, civil disobedience, poll tax, affirmative action, reverse discrimination, quota	**Teacher Notes**
PRETEACH	**RESOURCES**
___ **Before You Read . . .** (SE) Preview the Main Idea, Reading Focus, and Key Terms. ___ **Academic Vocabulary** (SE) Review with students the high-use academic terms in this section.	___ CRF: Vocabulary Builder: Section 3
DIRECT TEACH	**RESOURCES**
___ **Teach the Main Idea Activity** (TE) Students discuss the Reading Focus questions and create a list of the main ideas and events in this section. ___ **Primary Sources** (SE) "I Have a Dream" ___ **Collaborative Learning** (TE) Bus Boycott ___ **Differentiating Instruction: English-Language Learners** (TE) Federal Civil Rights Legislation **[Below Level]** ___ **Critical Thinking** (TE) Voting Rights Laws ___ **Differentiating Instruction: Special Needs Learners** (TE) Protest Songs **[Below Level]** ___ **Skills Focus** (TE) Affirmative Action Cartoons ___ **Debating the Issue** (TE, SE) Affirmative Action	___ Interactive Reader and Study Guide: Section 3 ___ CRF: Biography: Martin Luther King Jr. ___ CRF: Primary Source: Hamer on Civil Rights ___ Supreme Court Case Studies: Right to Treatment Cases, *University of California Regents* v. *Bakke*, Affirmative Action Cases
REVIEW & ASSESS	**RESOURCES**
___ **Close** (TE) Have students review the major federal civil rights laws passed during this period. ___ **Section 3 Assessment** (SE)	___ Online Quiz Section 3 keyword: SGO CRT HP ___ PASS: Section 3 Quiz

Key: SE = Student Edition **TE** = Teacher's Edition **CRF** = Chapter Resource File

Civil Rights

Lesson Plan

Section 4

Objectives Students will learn . . .	**Teacher Notes**
1. the ways in which people receive U.S. citizenship and what civic responsibilities citizens have.	
2. what immigration policies the federal government has adopted in its history.	
3. how the federal government responded to the challenge of illegal immigration.	
Key Terms Preteach the following terms: jus soli, jus sanguinis, naturalization, denaturalization, expatriation, undocumented alien, deportation	
PRETEACH	**RESOURCES**
___ **Before You Read . . .** (SE) Preview the Main Idea, Reading Focus, and Key Terms.	___ CRF: Vocabulary Builder: Section 4
___ **Academic Vocabulary** (SE) Review with students the high-use academic term in this section.	
DIRECT TEACH	**RESOURCES**
___ **Teach the Main Idea Activity** (TE) Students discuss the Reading Focus questions and write summaries focusing on citizenship, immigration policies, and illegal immigration.	___ Interactive Reader and Study Guide: Section 4
___ **Collaborative Learning** (TE) Responsibilities of Citizenship	___ Spanish/English Interactive Reader and Study Guide: Section 4
___ **Critical Thinking** (TE) Government Immigration Policies	___ CRF: Political Cartoon: Border Security
___ **Interpreting Graphs** (SE) Legal Immigration to the United States, 1820–2006	___ Supreme Court Case Studies: Terrorism Cases
___ **Differentiating Instruction: Struggling Readers** (TE) Immigration Policy Time Line **[Below Level]**	
___ **Critical Thinking** (TE) New Government Policies?	
___ **We the People** (TE, SE) Civic Participation	
REVIEW & ASSESS	**RESOURCES**
___ **Close** (TE) Have students discuss the different types of citizenship and the various government immigration policies and laws over the years.	___ Online Quiz Section 4 keyword: SGO CRT HP
___ **Section 4 Assessment** (SE)	___ PASS: Section 4 Quiz

Key: SE = Student Edition **TE** = Teacher's Edition **CRF** = Chapter Resource File

Understanding Elections

Lesson Plan
Section 1

Objectives Students will learn . . . 1. how election campaigns are planned and organized. 2. how candidates today use media exposure and polling to influence voters and get elected. **Key Terms** Preteach the following terms: platform, focus group, swing states, stump speech, negative campaigning, sound bite, demographic	**Teacher Notes**
PRETEACH	**RESOURCES**
___ **Teach the Reading Focus** (TE) Discuss with students the Reading Focus questions and have students identify the people involved in a political campaign. ___ **Using the Case Study** (TE) Television and the 1960 Election ___ **Academic Vocabulary** (SE) Review with students the high-use academic term in this section.	___ CRF: Vocabulary Builder: Section 1 ___ Student Casebook: Section 1: Case Study
DIRECT TEACH	**RESOURCES**
___ **Differentiating Instruction: English-Language Learners** (TE) Understanding Concepts **[Below Level]** ___ **Collaborative Learning** (TE) Forming a Campaign Team ___ **Critical Thinking** (TE) Issue Advisers ___ **Creative Thinking** (TE) The Candidate's Team ___ **Skills Focus** (TE) American Voters ___ **Collaborative Learning** (TE) Writing a Campaign Song	___ Interactive Reader and Study Guide: Section 1 ___ Student Casebook: Section 1: What You Need to Know ___ Transparency Quick Facts: The Campaign Team ___ CRF: Primary Source: A Presidential Debate
SIMULATION	**RESOURCES**
___ **Differentiating Instruction: Struggling Readers** (TE) Running a Presidential Campaign **[Below Level]** ___ **Responsibilities of Leadership** (TE) Supporting a Candidate	___ Student Casebook: Section 1: Student Simulation
REVIEW & ASSESS	**RESOURCES**
___ **Close** (TE) Have students share their view about political polling and how it affect the campaign process. ___ **Section 1 Assessment** (SE)	___ Online Quiz Section 1 keyword: SGO ELE HP ___ PASS: Section 1 Quiz

Key: SE = Student Edition **TE** = Teacher's Edition **CRF** = Chapter Resource File

Understanding Elections

Lesson Plan

Section 2

Objectives Students will learn . . . 1. how money plays a major role in election campaigns. 2. how candidates and their staff must decide where the campaign will get and how it will use money. **Key Terms** Preteach the following terms: Federal Election Commission, party-building activities, issue ads, leadership PACs, 527 group	**Teacher Notes**
PRETEACH	**RESOURCES**
___ **Teach the Reading Focus** (TE) Discuss with students the Reading Focus questions and have students identify the ways in which a campaign can raise money. ___ **Using the Case Study** (TE) Controversies over Campaign Funding ___ **Critical Thinking** (TE) Political Time Lines ___ **Academic Vocabulary** (SE) Review with students the high-use academic term in this section.	___ CRF: Vocabulary Builder: Section 2 ___ Student Casebook: Section 2: Case Study
DIRECT TEACH	**RESOURCES**
___ **Skills Focus** (TE) Senate Race Expenses ___ **Collaborative Learning** (TE) Debating Campaign Spending Restrictions ___ **Differentiating Instruction: Special Needs Learners** (TE) Political Parties **[Below Level]** ___ **Differentiating Instruction: Advanced/Gifted and Talented** (TE) Campaign Finance Reform Speeches ___ **Critical Thinking** (TE) PAC Interactions ___ **Collaborative Learning** (TE) Creating Issue Ads	___ Interactive Reader and Study Guide: Section 2 ___ Student Casebook: Section 2: What You Need to Know ___ Transparency: Political Cartoon: "It Takes a Village" ___ CRF: Primary Source: Russ Feingold
SIMULATION	**RESOURCES**
___ **Differentiating Instruction: English-Language Learners** (TE) Deciding to Back a Candidate ___ **Responsibilities of Leadership** (TE) Joining an Interest Group	___ Student Casebook: Section 2: Student Simulation
REVIEW & ASSESS	**RESOURCES**
___ **Close** (TE) Have students name the ways in which candidates fund their campaigns. ___ **Section 2 Assessment** (SE)	___ Online Quiz Section 2 keyword: SGO ELE HP ___ PASS: Section 2 Quiz

Key: SE = Student Edition **TE** = Teacher's Edition **CRF** = Chapter Resource File

Understanding Elections

Lesson Plan
Section 3

Objectives Students will learn . . . 1. why voting is one of the main responsibilities of U.S. citizenship. 2. how being part of the voting process gives Americans a voice in their government. **Key Terms** Preteach the following terms: poll workers, poll watchers, redistricting	**Teacher Notes**

PRETEACH	**RESOURCES**
___ **Teach the Reading Focus** (TE) Discuss with students the Reading Focus questions and have students identify the ways in which a campaign can raise money. ___ **Using the Case Study** (TE) Election 2000 ___ **Critical Thinking** (TE) Political Time Lines ___ **Academic Vocabulary** (SE) Review with students the high-use academic term in this section.	___ CRF: Vocabulary Builder: Section 3 ___ Student Casebook: Section 3: Case Study ___ Teacher One Stop™: Differentiated Instruction Modified Worksheets and Tests

DIRECT TEACH	**RESOURCES**
___ **Differentiating Instruction: English-Language Learners** (TE) Encouraging Young People to Vote ___ **Collaborative Learning** (TE) Encouraging Voter Participation ___ **Critical Thinking** (TE) Voting in Other Countries ___ **Skills Focus** (TE) Campaign Issues ___ **Skills Focus** (TE) Redistricting	___ Interactive Reader and Study Guide: Section 3 ___ Student Casebook: Section 3: What You Need to Know ___ CRF: Political Cartoon: Voter Turnout ___ Supreme Court Case Studies: *Bush* v. *Gore*

SIMULATION	**RESOURCES**
___ **Differentiating Instruction: Special Needs Learners** (TE) Planning Election Day Strategies ___ **Responsibilities of Leadership** (TE) Getting out the Vote	___ Student Casebook: Section 3: Student Simulation

REVIEW & ASSESS	**RESOURCES**
___ **Close** (TE) Have students discuss why it is important for citizens in a republic to vote. ___ **Section 3 Assessment** (SE)	___ Online Quiz Section 3 keyword: SGO ELE HP ___ PASS: Section 3 Quiz

Key: SE = Student Edition **TE** = Teacher's Edition **CRF** = Chapter Resource File

Supreme Court Cases

Lesson Plan

Section 1

Objectives Students will learn . . . 1. how religious freedom, freedom of speech, and the right to assemble are cornerstones of American democracy. 2. how the Supreme Court has expanded and limited Americans' freedom of expression. **Key Terms** Preteach the following terms: freedom of expression, redress of grievances, right of assembly	**Teacher Notes**
PRETEACH	**RESOURCES**
____ **Teach the Reading Focus** (TE) Discuss with students the Reading Focus questions and have students write a paragraph explaining the freedoms guaranteed by the First Amendment. ____ **Using the Case Study** (TE) Students' Right of Expression ____ **Collaborative Learning** (TE) Applying the Tinker Test ____ **Academic Vocabulary** (SE) Review with students the high-use academic term in this section.	____ CRF: Vocabulary Builder: Section 1 ____ Student Casebook: Section 1: Case Study
DIRECT TEACH	**RESOURCES**
____ **Critical Thinking** (TE) The Establishment Clause ____ **Differentiating Instruction: Struggling Readers** (TE) Concept Collage **[Below Level]** ____ **Skills Focus** (TE) The First Amendment ____ **Differentiating Instruction: English-Language Learners** (TE) Concept Cards **[Below Level]** ____ **Collaborative Learning** (TE) Writing a Speech Code ____ **Critical Thinking** (TE) Supreme Court Decisions	____ Interactive Reader and Study Guide: Section 1 ____ Transparencies: Quick Facts: Your First Amendment Freedoms, Religion in Public Places, Protected and Unprotected Speech
SIMULATION	**RESOURCES**
____ **Differentiating Instruction: Struggling Readers** (TE) The Play's the Thing **[Below Level]** ____ **Responsibilities of Leadership** (TE) The First Amendment at School	____ Student Casebook: Section 1: Student Simulation
REVIEW & ASSESS	**RESOURCES**
____ **Close** (TE) Have students list Supreme Court cases relating to the First Amendment. ____ **Section 1 Assessment** (SE)	____ Online Quiz Section 1 keyword: SGO SUP HP ____ PASS: Section 1 Quiz

Key: SE = Student Edition **TE** = Teacher's Edition **CRF** = Chapter Resource File

Supreme Court Cases

Lesson Plan

Section 2

Objectives Students will learn . . . 1. how the Fourth Amendment provides protections against searches and seizures made by the government. 2. what rulings the Supreme Court has made with regard to protecting the right to privacy. **Key Terms** Preteach the following terms: freedom of search, seizure, plain view doctrine, Terry stop, special needs test, cyber-surveillance, National Security letter	**Teacher Notes**
PRETEACH	**RESOURCES**
____ **Teach the Reading Focus** (TE) Discuss with students the Reading Focus questions and have students make a list of methods used to conduct searches. ____ **Using the Case Study** (TE) The Right to Privacy ____ **Collaborative Learning** (TE) Illegal Searches	____ CRF: Vocabulary Builder: Section 2 ____ Student Casebook: Section 2: Case Study
DIRECT TEACH	**RESOURCES**
____ **Differentiating Instruction: Struggling Readers** (TE) Writing Quiz Questions **[Below Level]** ____ **Collaborative Learning** (TE) Lawful Search and Seizure ____ **Differentiating Instruction: Advanced/Gifted and Talented** (TE) Researching the Fourth Amendment **[Above Level]** ____ **Critical Thinking** (TE) Privacy Rights ____ **Critical Thinking** (TE) Privacy Issues ____ **Critical Thinking** (TE) Right to Privacy Cases	____ Interactive Reader and Study Guide: Section 2 ____ Student Casebook: Section 2: What You Need to Know ____ Transparency: Quick Facts: Warrantless Searches ____ Transparency: Quick Facts: Terry Stop
SIMULATION	**RESOURCES**
____ **Differentiating Instruction: English-Language Learners** (TE) Have You Been Seized? **[Below Level]** ____ **Responsibilities of Leadership** (TE) Writing an Amicus Curiae Brief	____ Student Casebook: Section 2: Student Simulation
REVIEW & ASSESS	**RESOURCES**
____ **Close** (TE) Have students discuss the fluctuating nature of Fourth Amendment privacy rights. ____ **Section 2 Assessment** (SE)	____ Online Quiz Section 2 keyword: SGO SUP HP ____ PASS: Section 2 Quiz

Key: **SE** = Student Edition **TE** = Teacher's Edition **CRF** = Chapter Resource File

Supreme Court Cases

Lesson Plan

Section 3

Objectives Students will learn . . .	Teacher Notes
1. how the Fourteenth Amendment provides due process and equal protection for all Americans. 2. how the Supreme Court has used substantive due process to decide what unenumerated rights people have. 3. how the Supreme Court has expanded procedural due process over the years. **Key Terms** Preteach the following term: unenumerated rights	

PRETEACH	**RESOURCES**
___ **Teach the Reading Focus** (TE) Discuss with students the Reading Focus questions and have students write a newspaper editorial about due process rights. ___ **Using the Case Study** (TE) Due Process and Public Schools	___ CRF: Vocabulary Builder: Section 3 ___ Student Casebook: Section 3: Case Study

DIRECT TEACH	**RESOURCES**
___ **Collaborative Learning** (TE) The Fourteenth Amendment ___ **Critical Thinking** (TE) Procedural and Substantive Due Process ___ **Critical Thinking** (TE) Freedom to Work ___ **Differentiating Instruction: English-Language Learners** (TE) Writing Sentences **[Below Level]** ___ **Collaborative Learning** (TE) The Right to Die ___ **Differentiating Instruction: Special Needs Learners** (TE) Illustrating Procedural Due Process **[Below Level]**	___ Interactive Reader and Study Guide: Section 3 ___ Student Casebook: Section 3: What You Need to Know ___ Transparency: Quick Facts: Procedural Due Process ___ Transparency: Quick Facts: Substantive Due Process

SIMULATION	**RESOURCES**
___ **Differentiating Instruction: Struggling Readers** (TE) Terrorists and Due Process **[Below Level]** ___ **Responsibilities of Leadership** (TE) Championing Due Process Rights	___ Student Casebook: Section 3: Student Simulation

REVIEW & ASSESS	**RESOURCES**
___ **Close** (TE) Have students discuss the differences between procedural and substantive due process. ___ **Section 3 Assessment** (SE)	___ Online Quiz Section 3 keyword: SGO SUP HP ___ PASS: Section 3 Quiz

Key: SE = Student Edition **TE** = Teacher's Edition **CRF** = Chapter Resource File

Supreme Court Cases

Lesson Plan

Section 4

	Teacher Notes
Objectives Students will learn . . . 1. how federal authority has increased over the years at the expense of the states. 2. how the Supreme Court has used the commerce clause to expand federal authority. **Key Terms** Preteach the following term: selective exclusiveness	

PRETEACH	**RESOURCES**
____ **Teach the Reading Focus** (TE) Discuss with students the Reading Focus questions and have students create an outline of this section. ____ **Using the Case Study** (TE) Treaties and States' Rights	____ CRF: Vocabulary Builder: Section 4 ____ Student Casebook: Section 4: Case Study

DIRECT TEACH	**RESOURCES**
____ **Differentiating Instruction: Advanced/Gifted and Talented** (TE) Researching *Gibbons* v. *Ogden* **[Above Level]** ____ **Critical Thinking** (TE) Interstate Commerce ____ **Collaborative Learning** (TE) Issuing a Decision	____ Interactive Reader and Study Guide: Section 4 ____ Student Casebook: Section 4: What You Need to Know ____ CRF: Primary Source: *Bush* v. *Gore* ____ CRF: Economics and Government: Supreme Court and Trade

SIMULATION	**RESOURCES**
____ **Differentiating Instruction: English-Language Learners** (TE) Arguing a Federalism Case **[Below Level]** ____ **Responsibilities of Leadership** (TE) Circulating a Petition	____ Student Casebook: Section 4: Student Simulation

REVIEW & ASSESS	**RESOURCES**
____ **Close** (TE) Have students make a list of five activities that affect interstate commerce and five activities that do not affect interstate commerce. ____ **Section 4 Assessment** (SE)	____ Online Quiz Section 4 keyword: SGO SUP HP ____ PASS: Section 4 Quiz

Key: SE = Student Edition **TE** = Teacher's Edition **CRF** = Chapter Resource File

Making Foreign Policy

Lesson Plan

Section 1

Objectives Students will learn . . .	**Teacher Notes**
1. what five basic goals guide U.S. foreign policy.	
2. what foreign policy tools the United States uses.	
3. what the just war theory is.	
Key Terms Preteach the following terms: foreign policy, isolationism, internationalist, embassies, defense alliance, collective security, economic sanctions, just war theory	

PRETEACH	RESOURCES
___ **Teach the Reading Focus** (TE) Discuss with students the Reading Focus questions and have students take notes on the goals and tools of foreign policy.	___ CRF: Vocabulary Builder: Section 1
___ **Using the Case Study** (TE) Genocide in Rwanda	___ Student Casebook: Section 1 Case Study
___ **Academic Vocabulary** (SE) Review with students the high-use academic term in this section.	

DIRECT TEACH	RESOURCES
___ **Differentiating Instruction: English-Language Learners** (TE) Understanding Concepts **[Below Level]**	___ Interactive Reader and Study Guide: Section 1
___ **Collaborative Learning** (TE) Foreign Policy Goals	___ Student Casebook: Section 1 What You Need to Know
___ **Critical Thinking** (TE) International Organizations	
___ **Collaborative Learning** (TE) Debating Sanctions	___ Transparency Quick Facts: Major U.S. Defense Alliances
___ **Interpreting Charts** (SE) Structure and Control of the U.S. Military	
___ **Differentiating Instruction: Special Needs Learners** (TE) Researching the U.S. Military **[Below Level]**	

SIMULATION	RESOURCES
___ **Differentiating Instruction: Struggling Readers** (TE) Understanding Foreign Policy Goals **[Below Level]**	___ Student Casebook: Section 1 Student Simulation
___ **Responsibilities of Leadership** (TE) Influencing Foreign Policy	

REVIEW & ASSESS	RESOURCES
___ **Close** (TE) Have students discuss how the words *continuity* and *change* apply to U.S. foreign policy.	___ Online Quiz Section 1 keyword: SGO FOR HP
___ **Section 1 Assessment** (SE)	___ PASS: Section 1 Quiz

Key: SE = Student Edition **TE** = Teacher's Edition **CRF** = Chapter Resource File

Making Foreign Policy

Lesson Plan
Section 2

Objectives Students will learn . . . 1. what role the federal bureaucracy plays in making U.S. foreign policy. 2. how Congress and the president direct foreign policy. 3. how interest groups help shape U.S. foreign policy. **Key Terms** Preteach the following terms: foreign service, presidential doctrines, diplomatic recognition	**Teacher Notes**

PRETEACH	**RESOURCES**
____ **Teach the Reading Focus** (TE) Discuss with students the Reading Focus questions and have students create a flowchart illustrating the relationships among foreign policy actors. ____ **Using the Case Study** (TE) Elián González ____ **Collaborative Learning** (TE) The Elián González Controversy ____ **Academic Vocabulary** (SE) Review with students the high-use academic term in this section.	____ CRF: Vocabulary Builder: Section 2 ____ Student Casebook: Section 2 Case Study

DIRECT TEACH	**RESOURCES**
____ **Differentiating Instruction: Struggling Readers** (TE) Foreign Policy Bureaucracy **[Below Level]** ____ **Critical Thinking** (TE) Foreign Policy Crises ____ **Skills Focus** (TE) Presidential Responsibilities ____ **Critical Thinking** (TE) Presidential Roles ____ **Differentiating Instruction: English-Language Learners** (TE) Political Cartoon **[Below Level]**	____ Interactive Reader and Study Guide: Section 2 ____ Student Casebook: Section 2 What You Need to Know ____ Transparency Quick Facts: Foreign Policy Bureaucracy

SIMULATION	**RESOURCES**
____ **Differentiating Instruction: Struggling Readers** (TE) Senate Trade Bill Vote **[Below Level]** ____ **Responsibilities of Leadership** (TE) Influencing Foreign Policy	____ Student Casebook: Section 2 Student Simulation

REVIEW & ASSESS	**RESOURCES**
____ **Close** (TE) Have students write a paragraph explaining who shapes and influences U.S. foreign policy. ____ **Section 2 Assessment** (SE)	____ Online Quiz Section 2 keyword: SGO FOR HP ____ PASS: Section 2 Quiz

Key: SE = Student Edition **TE** = Teacher's Edition **CRF** = Chapter Resource File

Making Foreign Policy

Lesson Plan

Section 3

Objectives Students will learn . . . 1. how the United Nations works to maintain peace and political stability throughout the world. 2. how other international institutions help govern the world's economic and judicial systems. **Key Terms** Preteach the following terms: UN Security Council, trust territory	**Teacher Notes**
PRETEACH	**RESOURCES**
____ **Teach the Reading Focus** (TE) Discuss with students the Reading Focus questions and have students identify international organizations and parts of the UN. ____ **Using the Case Study** (TE) Making the Case for War ____ **Skills Focus** (TE) Reaching International Consensus ____ **Academic Vocabulary** (SE) Review with students the high-use academic term in this section.	____ CRF: Vocabulary Builder: Section 3 ____ Student Casebook: Section 3 Case Study
DIRECT TEACH	**RESOURCES**
____ **Differentiating Instruction: English-Language Learners** (TE) Joining the UN **[At Level]** ____ **Collaborative Learning** (TE) Goals of the UN ____ **Differentiating Instruction: Advanced/Gifted and Talented** (TE) Writing Biographies **[Above Level]** ____ **Critical Thinking** (TE) International Criminal Court	____ Interactive Reader and Study Guide: Section 3 ____ Student Casebook: Section 3 What You Need to Know ____ CRF: Primary Source: Universal Declaration of Human Rights
SIMULATION	**RESOURCES**
____ **Differentiating Instruction: Special Needs Learners** (TE) Crisis at the UN Security Council **[Below Level]** ____ **Responsibilities of Leadership** (TE) Influencing Foreign Policy	____ Student Casebook: Section 3 Student Simulation
REVIEW & ASSESS	**RESOURCES**
____ **Close** (TE) Create a class list of international organizations of which the United States is a member. ____ **Section 3 Assessment** (SE)	____ Online Quiz Section 3 keyword: SGO FOR HP ____ PASS: Section 3 Quiz

Key: SE = Student Edition TE = Teacher's Edition CRF = Chapter Resource File

Making Foreign Policy

Lesson Plan

Section 4

Objectives Students will learn . . . 1. what major shifts in foreign policy the United States has experienced. 2. what contemporary foreign policy challenges the United States faces. **Key Terms** Preteach the following terms: Monroe Doctrine, deterrence, containment, détente, preemptive strike, democratization, food security.	**Teacher Notes**
PRETEACH	**RESOURCES**
___ **Teach the Reading Focus** (TE) Discuss with students the Reading Focus questions and have students map regions in which the United States has experienced foreign policy challenges. ___ **Using the Case Study** (TE) The Czech Republic ___ **Academic Vocabulary** (SE) Review with students the high-use academic term in this section.	___ CRF: Vocabulary Builder: Section 4 ___ Student Casebook: Section 4 Case Study
DIRECT TEACH	**RESOURCES**
___ **Differentiating Instruction: English-Language Learners** (TE) Vocabulary **[Below Level]** ___ **Critical Thinking** (TE) Foreign Policy Decisions ___ **Differentiating Instruction: Struggling Readers** (TE) Reading about Foreign Policy **[At Level]** ___ **Critical Thinking** (TE) The Cold War Flowchart ___ **Collaborative Learning** (TE) Current Foreign Policy ___ **Critical Thinking** (TE) Struggles for Democracy	___ Interactive Reader and Study Guide: Section 4 ___ Student Casebook: Section 4 What You Need to Know ___ CRF: Biographies: Pope John Paul II and Lech Walesa
SIMULATION	**RESOURCES**
___ **Differentiating Instruction: Struggling Readers** (TE) Negotiating an Environmental Treaty **[Below Level]** ___ **Responsibilities of Leadership** (TE) Taking Responsibility for the Environment	___ Student Casebook: Section 4 Student Simulation
REVIEW & ASSESS	**RESOURCES**
___ **Close** (TE) Have students create a list of major foreign policy challenges the United States faces today. ___ **Section 4 Assessment** (SE)	___ Online Quiz Section 4 keyword: SGO FOR HP ___ PASS: Section 4 Quiz

Key: SE = Student Edition **TE** = Teacher's Edition **CRF** = Chapter Resource File

Comparative Political and Economic Systems   Lesson Plan

Section 1

	Teacher Notes
Objectives Students will learn . . . 1. how different types of democratic systems are organized. 2. how presidential democracies and parliamentary democracies are similar and different. 3. how some countries are slowly moving toward democratic governments. **Key Terms** Preteach the following terms: authoritarian, coalition, apartheid	

PRETEACH	**RESOURCES**
___ **Teach the Reading Focus** (TE) Discuss with students the Reading Focus questions and have students explain the different types of democracy. ___ **Using the Case Study** (TE) Emerging Democracy in Nigeria ___ **Academic Vocabulary** (SE) Review with students the high-use academic terms in this section.	___ CRF: Vocabulary Builder: Section 1 ___ Student Casebook: Section 1: Case Study

DIRECT TEACH	**RESOURCES**
___ **Differentiating Instruction: English-Language Learners** (TE) Understanding Vocabulary ___ **Critical Thinking** (TE) Selected or Elected? ___ **Differentiating Instruction: Special Needs Learners** (TE) Celebrating Democracy **[Below Level]** ___ **Differentiating Instruction: Advanced/Gifted and Talented** (TE) Multimedia Presentation **[Above Level]** ___ **Critical Thinking** (TE) Ceremonial Leaders ___ **Skills Focus** (TE) Gaining Independence	___ Interactive Reader and Study Guide: Section 1 ___ Student Casebook: Section 1: What You Need to Know ___ CRF: Primary Source: Bachelet on Chile's Future ___ CRF: Primary Source: Mandela on Apartheid

SIMULATION	**RESOURCES**
___ **Differentiating Instruction: Struggling Readers** (TE) Choosing a System of Government **[Below Level]** ___ **Responsibilities of Leadership** (TE) Supporting Democracy	___ Student Casebook: Section 1: Student Simulation

REVIEW & ASSESS	**RESOURCES**
___ **Close** (TE) Have students identify and describe one presidential and one parliamentary democracy. ___ **Section 1 Assessment** (SE)	___ Online Quiz Section 1 keyword: SGO PES HP ___ PASS: Section 1 Quiz

Key: SE = Student Edition **TE** = Teacher's Edition **CRF** = Chapter Resource File

Comparative Political and Economic Systems Lesson Plan

Section 2

Objectives Students will learn . . .	**Teacher Notes**
1. what types of authoritarian systems exist and how they are organized.	
2. the nature of authoritarian governments in the Soviet Union and China.	
3. how authoritarian systems function in other countries.	
Key Terms Preteach the following terms: theocracy, totalitarianism, communism	

PRETEACH	**RESOURCES**
____ **Teach the Reading Focus** (TE) Discuss with students the Reading Focus questions and have students list characteristics and examples of authoritarian governments. ____ **Using the Case Study** (TE) Totalitarian Rule in North Korea	____ CRF: Vocabulary Builder: Section 2 ____ Student Casebook: Section 2: Case Study

DIRECT TEACH	**RESOURCES**
____ **Differentiating Instruction: Struggling Readers** (TE) Describing Authoritarian Systems **[Below Level]** ____ **Critical Thinking** (TE) Authoritarian Governments ____ **Critical Thinking** (TE) Religious Intolerance ____ **Differentiating Instruction: English-Language Learners** (TE) Creating Time Lines **[Below Level]** ____ **Differentiating Instruction: Advanced/Gifted and Talented** (TE) Examining Saudi Arabia **[Above Level]**	____ Interactive Reader and Study Guide: Section 2 ____ Student Casebook: Section 2: What You Need to Know ____ Transparency: Quick Facts: Characteristics of Authoritarian Systems ____ CRF: Biography: Aung San Suu Kyi

SIMULATION	**RESOURCES**
____ **Differentiating Instruction: Struggling Readers** (TE) Overthrowing a Dictator **[Below Level]** ____ **Responsibilities of Leadership** (TE) Helping Victims of Oppression	____ Student Casebook: Section 2: Student Simulation

REVIEW & ASSESS	**RESOURCES**
____ **Close** (TE) Have students compare and contrast authoritarian governments around the world. ____ **Section 2 Assessment** (SE)	____ Online Quiz Section 2 keyword: SGO PES HP ____ PASS: Section 2 Quiz

Key: SE = Student Edition **TE** = Teacher's Edition **CRF** = Chapter Resource File

Comparative Political and Economic Systems   Lesson Plan

	Teacher Notes
Objectives Students will learn . . . 1. how societies and countries make economic decisions. 2. what the three types of mixed economies are and how they each function. **Key Terms** Preteach the following terms: factors of production, traditional economy, market economy, command economy, mixed economy, capitalism, laissez-faire, socialism, proletariat, bourgeoisie	

PRETEACH	RESOURCES
____ **Teach the Reading Focus** (TE) Discuss with students the Reading Focus questions and have students identify the different economic systems. ____ **Using the Case Study** (TE) A Changing India ____ **Academic Vocabulary** (SE) Review with students the high-use academic term in this section.	____ CRF: Vocabulary Builder: Section 3 ____ Student Casebook: Section 3: Case Study

DIRECT TEACH	RESOURCES
____ **Skills Focus** (TE) Economic Systems ____ **Differentiating Instruction: English-Language Learners** (TE) Writing Quiz Questions **[Below Level]** ____ **Critical Thinking** (TE) Philosophical Theories ____ **Critical Thinking** (TE) Writing a Song or Poem ____ **Differentiating Instruction: Struggling Readers** (TE) Communist Propaganda **[Below Level]**	____ Interactive Reader and Study Guide: Section 3 ____ Student Casebook: Section 3: What You Need to Know ____ Transparencies: Quick Facts: Types of Economic Systems, Factors of Production ____ CRF: Biography: Adam Smith

SIMULATION	RESOURCES
____ **Differentiating Instruction: Special Needs Learners** (TE) Negotiating a Trade Agreement **[Below Level]** ____ **Responsibilities of Leadership** (TE) Supporting or Opposing a Trade Agreement	____ Student Casebook: Section 3: Student Simulation

REVIEW & ASSESS	RESOURCES
____ **Close** (TE) Have students list characteristics of the three basic economic systems. ____ **Section 3 Assessment** (SE)	____ Online Quiz Section 3 keyword: SGO PES HP ____ PASS: Section 3 Quiz

Key: SE = Student Edition **TE** = Teacher's Edition **CRF** = Chapter Resource File

State and Local Government

Lesson Plan

Section 1

Objectives Students will learn . . .	Teacher Notes
1. what the relationship is between state governments and the national government. 2. the characteristics of state constitutions. **Key Terms** Preteach the following terms: guarantee clause, fundamental law, statutory law	

PRETEACH	RESOURCES
___ **Teach the Reading Focus** (TE) Discuss with students the Reading Focus questions and have students identify similarities and differences between the U.S. Constitution and state constitutions. ___ **Primary Source** (TE) Sovereignty of the States ___ **Using the Case Study** (TE) The Nullification Crisis	___ CRF: Vocabulary Builder: Section 1 ___ Student Casebook: Section 1 Case Study

DIRECT TEACH	RESOURCES
___ **Critical Thinking** (TE) Federalism and the States ___ **Differentiating Instruction: Advanced/Gifted and Talented** (TE) Researching State Constitutions [Above Level] ___ **Skills Focus** (TE) Amending the Constitution	___ Interactive Reader and Study Guide: Section 1 ___ Student Casebook: Section 1 What You Need to Know ___ Transparency Quick Facts: Characteristics of State Constitutions ___ Transparency: Quick Facts: Constitutions and Amendments

SIMULATION	RESOURCES
___ **Differentiating Instruction: English-Language Learners** (TE) Amending the State Constitution [At Level] ___ **Responsibilities of Leadership** (TE) Writing to a Member of the State Legislature	___ Student Casebook: Section 1 Student Simulation

REVIEW & ASSESS	RESOURCES
___ **Close** (TE) Have students discuss how state constitutions reflect the principles of federalism. ___ **Section 1 Assessment** (SE)	___ Online Quiz Section 1 keyword: SGO SLG HP ___ PASS: Section 1 Quiz

Key: SE = Student Edition **TE** = Teacher's Edition **CRF** = Chapter Resource File

State and Local Government

Lesson Plan

Section 2

Objectives Students will learn . . .
 	
  1. how state governments are organized.
 	
  2. the types of state legislatures and their functions.
 	
  3. the characteristics of state executive branches.
 	
  4. the organization and responsibilities of state judiciaries.
 	
Key Terms Preteach the following terms: governor, citizen legislatures, professional legislatures, line-item veto, executive clemency, Missouri Plan
	Teacher Notes

PRETEACH	**RESOURCES**
___ **Teach the Reading Focus** (TE) Discuss with students the Reading Focus questions and have students create a graphic organizer illustrating the division of power in state governments. ___ **Using the Case Study** (TE) Teen Driving Laws ___ **Academic Vocabulary** (SE) Review with students the high-use academic terms in this section	___ CRF: Vocabulary Builder: Section 2 ___ Student Casebook: Section 2 Case Study
DIRECT TEACH	**RESOURCES**
___ **Differentiating Instruction: Special Needs Learners** (TE) Examining State Flags **[Below Level]** ___ **Critical Thinking** (TE) Comparing States ___ **Skills Focus** (TE) Creating a New State Legislature ___ **Skills Focus** (TE) Redistricting ___ **Critical Thinking** (TE) Serving as Governor ___ **Critical Thinking** (TE) Public Policy Issues ___ **Interpreting Charts** (SE) State Government Finances	___ Interactive Reader and Study Guide: Section 2 ___ Student Casebook: Section 2 What You Need to Know ___ Transparencies Quick Facts: State Legislatures, The Governorship
SIMULATION	**RESOURCES**
___ **Differentiating Instruction: Special Needs Learners** (TE) Budgeting and Public Policy **[Below Level]** ___ **Responsibilities of Leadership** (TE) Influencing State Government	___ Student Casebook: Section 2 Student Simulation
REVIEW & ASSESS	**RESOURCES**
___ **Close** (TE) Have students list the ways in which state governments are similar to the federal government. ___ **Section 2 Assessment** (SE)	___ Online Quiz Section 2 keyword: SGO SLG HP ___ PASS: Section 2 Quiz

Key: SE = Student Edition **TE** = Teacher's Edition **CRF** = Chapter Resource File

State and Local Government

Lesson Plan
Section 3

Objectives Students will learn . . . 1. how local governments are organized and what services they provide. 2. how individuals participate in local government. **Key Terms** Preteach the following terms: counties, parishes, boroughs, townships, municipalities, incorporation, mayor-council system, council-manager system, commission system, special districts, zoning laws, initiative, referendum, recall	**Teacher Notes**
PRETEACH	**RESOURCES**
____ **Teach the Reading Focus** (TE) Discuss with students the Reading Focus questions and have students list the different types of local governments. ____ **Using the Case Study** (TE) Land Use in Easton, Maryland	____ CRF: Vocabulary Builder: Section 3 ____ Student Casebook: Section 3 Case Study
DIRECT TEACH	**RESOURCES**
____ **Differentiating Instruction: Struggling Readers** (TE) Local Government Posters **[Below Level]** ____ **Biography** (TE) Martin J. Chávez ____ **Critical Thinking** (TE) Comparing Local Governments ____ **Primary Source** (TE) California Governor Arnold Schwarzenegger ____ **Interpreting Charts** (SE) Local Government Finances ____ **Collaborative Learning** (TE) Urban Sprawl	____ Interactive Reader and Study Guide: Section 3 ____ Spanish/English Interactive Reader and Study Guide: Section 3 ____ Student Casebook: Section 3 What You Need to Know ____ CRF: Biography: Robert Morgenthau
SIMULATION	**RESOURCES**
____ **Differentiating Instruction: Struggling Readers** (TE) Conducting the City's Business ____ **Responsibilities of Leadership** (TE) Attending a Council Meeting	____ Student Casebook: Section 3 Student Simulation
REVIEW & ASSESS	**RESOURCES**
____ **Close** (TE) Have students discuss whether their own local government is typical of other local governments. ____ **Section 3 Assessment** (SE)	____ Online Quiz Section 3 keyword: SGO SLG HP ____ PASS: Section 3 Quiz

Key: SE = Student Edition **TE** = Teacher's Edition **CRF** = Chapter Resource File

Lesson Plans for
Differentiated Instruction

Section 1: The Purposes of Government

SUPPORTING ENGLISH-LANGUAGE INSTRUCTION

Prereading (10 minutes)

Preparing an Outline Have students look at the section and use the main heads and run-in heads to prepare an outline structure. Have students look for other important information such as key terms or concepts that they might include as a subtopic or supporting detail. For example, the caption "Sources of Power" should indicate to students an important subtopic to include in their outlines. Remind students that they are only preparing the outline structure. They will complete the outline in the next step.

Reading (30 minutes)

Creating an Outline Using the outline structure students prepared as part of the prereading stage, have students read the section and complete the outline. You may want to have students work in pairs to fill in their outlines. As students read the section, have them complete the outline with key information about the purposes of government. Remind students that an outline contains the main ideas from the section along with any supporting details. These details are indented to show their relationship to the main ideas.

Section 2: Forms of Government

SUPPORTING SPECIAL EDUCATION INSTRUCTION

Understanding Information (30 minutes)

Comparing Different Ways of Organizing National Power As students read the text under the heading "Organizing National Power," point out to them the three main systems of organizing national power—unitary, federal, and confederal. Have students use their own sheet of paper to create a graphic organizer like the one at right. As students review each system, have them write down the characteristics of each system in the graphic organizer. Then have students create an illustration or symbol that represents each system of government. You may want to have students work in pairs or small groups to develop their illustrations.

Resources

- Spanish Chapter Summaries Audio CD Program

- Differentiated Instruction Modified Worksheets and Tests on the Teacher's One Stop™
  – Vocabulary Flash Cards
  – Vocabulary Activities
  – Chapter Review
  – Section Quizzes
  – Chapter Test

- Advanced Placement Review and Activities

Vocabulary Tip

As this section explains, the term *state* is used throughout the chapter to refer not to one of the 50 states, but to a political unit similar to a country or nation-state.

Graphic Organizer

Systems of National Government		
Unitary	Federal	Confederal

SUPPORTING ADVANCED/GIFTED AND TALENTED INSTRUCTION

Expanding Information (40 minutes)

Classic Forms of Government around the World

Have students review the chart titled "Classic Forms of Government." Instruct each student to select one form of government to research. Then have each student identify a country that practices the form of government he or she selected. Have students use the library, Internet, or other sources to research information about the government of their selected countries. Students should include details such as the type of ruler, the ruler's name, the branches of government, and other characteristics of the government. Ask for volunteers to share their findings with the class.

Section 3: Democracy in the United States

SUPPORTING SPECIAL EDUCATION INSTRUCTION

Analyzing Information (30 minutes)

Supporting a Main Idea Have students begin by reading the main idea in the Before You Read portion of the section. Working in pairs or small groups, students will restate the main idea in their own words. Have students write the restated main idea at the top of a Main Ideas and Details chart like the one at right. Have students continue to work in pairs or small groups to locate supporting details in the section and place them in the chart.

SUPPORTING ENGLISH-LANGUAGE INSTRUCTION

Visualizing Information (30 minutes)

Understanding the Ideals of American Democracy

Have students read the text under the heading "Ideals of American Democracy." Then ask students to identify the three ideals mentioned in the text. Help students to understand the meaning of each of the three ideals. Then have students work together in pairs to draw images that best symbolize each of the ideals. For example, students may draw a picture of a person placing a ballot in a ballot box to represent the ideal of self-government. Encourage students to share their work with the class.

Graphic Organizer

Main Ideas and Details Chart

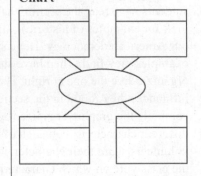

Section 1: The Roots of American Democracy

SUPPORTING ENGLISH-LANGUAGE INSTRUCTION

Expanding Information (45 minutes)

Researching Colonial Democracies Have students read the text under the heading "The English Colonies." Organize the class into 13 small groups and assign each group a different colony. Have students work together as a group to research the government of their assigned colony, focusing on the colony's democratic elements. Instruct each group to prepare a 5- to 10-minute presentation that explains its colony's government and democratic characteristics. Have each group give its presentation to the class. Encourage students to take notes on each presentation.

SUPPORTING SPECIAL EDUCATION INSTRUCTION

Analyzing Information (30 minutes)

Identifying Influences on American Democracy After students have read the section, have them skim the section to look for examples of historical influences that helped shape our American democracy. Have students make a list of the examples they find. Then have students create a graphic organizer like the one at right. Have students select four of the influences they found in the section. Instruct students to complete the graphic organizer by writing an explanation of a different characteristic in each of the outer circles. Have volunteers share their characteristics with the class. Then have the class vote on which characteristic had the greatest influence on the development of our government.

Section 2: American Independence

SUPPORTING SPECIAL EDUCATION INSTRUCTION

Sequencing Information (30 minutes)

Creating a Time Line As students read the section, have them list the key events that led to the American colonies' declaration of independence. Then have students create a time line using the events from their list. Remind students to include the date of each event and to list the events chronologically.

Resources

- Spanish Chapter Summaries Audio CD Program

- Differentiated Instruction Modified Worksheets and Tests on the Teacher One Stop™
  - Vocabulary Flash Cards
  - Vocabulary Activities
  - Chapter Review
  - Section Quizzes
  - Chapter Test

- Advanced Placement Review and Activities

Graphic Organizer

Roots of American Democracy

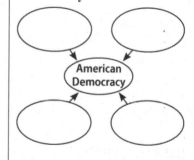

Teacher Tip

Have students who complete their time lines early create illustrations for several key events.

SUPPORTING ADVANCED/GIFTED AND TALENTED INSTRUCTION

Summarizing Information (30 minutes)

Examining the Declaration of Independence Have students read and take notes on the Declaration of Independence. Then instruct students to write a summary of the document in their own words. Have students write two to three clear and succinct sentences that summarize each paragraph. Have students share their summaries with the class.

Section 3: Articles of Confederation

SUPPORTING SPECIAL EDUCATION INSTRUCTION

Analyzing Information (30 minutes)

Understanding Cause and Effect Have students read the text under the headings "Weaknesses of the Articles" and "Pressures for Stronger Government." Have students make a list of the weaknesses of the Articles of Confederation as they read. Then have students create a graphic organizer like the one at right on their own sheet of paper. Instruct students to list each of the weaknesses in the boxes on the left. Then have students identify the results of those weaknesses in the boxes on the right. You may want to walk students through the weakness listed in the graphic organizer as an example.

Graphic Organizer
Weaknesses of the Articles of Confederation

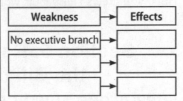

SUPPORTING ENGLISH-LANGUAGE INSTRUCTION

Summarizing Information (45 minutes)

Making a Persuasive Speech Have students reread the text under the heading "Pressures for Stronger Government." Discuss with the class why many Americans wanted to revise the government under the Articles of Confederation. Have students work with a partner to create two lists—one with reasons for keeping the Articles of Confederation without any changes and another list with reasons for changing the Articles of Confederation. Have each partner select a list and use it to write a persuasive speech in favor of his or her stance. Ask for volunteers to give their speeches to the class.

Teacher Tip
After all the speeches have been presented, ask students which arguments were most persuasive and why.

Section 4: The Constitutional Convention

SUPPORTING SPECIAL EDUCATION INSTRUCTION

Expanding Information (45 minutes)

Biographies of the Framers After students have read the section, discuss with them the pivotal role played by the delegates to the Constitutional Convention. Then have each student select a delegate to research. Instruct students to use the library, Internet, or other sources to find information about the person they selected. Students should look for information regarding that person's family, background, education, experience, and attitudes during the Convention. Have students write a short biography on the Framer they selected. Have volunteers share their work with the class.

Teacher Tip

Encourage students to find a quote by or about the person they selected. One source might be James Madison's journal of the Constitutional Convention.

Section 5: Ratification and the Bill of Rights

SUPPORTING ADVANCED/GIFTED AND TALENTED INSTRUCTION

Analyzing Information (45 minutes)

Debating the Constitution Have students skim the section, taking notes on the arguments used by the Federalists and the Antifederalists. Then organize the class for a debate on the following proposition: *The Constitution should not be adopted because it limits the power of the states*. Instruct each student to take a side in the debate and to conduct research in support of his or her stance. Then have students stage an orderly debate in class. After the debate, take a poll to see which arguments students thought were most persuasive and why.

Graphic Organizer
Debating Ratification

Arguments For	Arguments Against

Section 1: A Blueprint for Government

SUPPORTING SPECIAL EDUCATION INSTRUCTION

Summarizing Information (30 minutes)
Examining the Principles of the Constitution Start by organizing students into six groups. Assign each group a different principle of the Constitution. Have each group reread the portion of the section that deals with their assigned principle. Then have each group work together to create a poster that summarizes the main ideas behind its assigned principle. Encourage groups to use key vocabulary and concepts from the section on their posters. Have each group share its poster with the class. You may want to have the class take notes on the key points of each group's poster.

SUPPORTING ENGLISH-LANGUAGE INSTRUCTION

Expanding Information (45 minutes)
Understanding Checks and Balances Review with the class the concept of checks and balances. Discuss some of the key checks and balances, such as vetoes, Congressional approval of presidential appointments, and judicial review. Check to make sure that students understand the concept of checks and balances. Then have students search newspaper, magazine, or Internet articles for specific instances in which the different branches have used checks and balances. Encourage students to share their findings with the class.

Section 2: An Enduring Document

SUPPORTING SPECIAL EDUCATION INSTRUCTION

Organizing Information (30 minutes)
Sequencing Events Review with the class the process for amending the Constitution. Then have students work in small groups to create a graphic organizer or flowchart that illustrates the sequence of events necessary to amend the Constitution. Have students create their organizer or flowchart on butcher paper or poster board. Have each group display its diagram for everyone to see.

Resources

- Spanish Chapter Summaries Audio CD Program
- Differentiated Instruction Modified Worksheets and Tests on the Teacher's One Stop™
  – Vocabulary Flash Cards
  – Vocabulary Activities
  – Chapter Review
  – Section Quizzes
  – Chapter Test
- Advanced Placement Review and Activities

Vocabulary Tip

Explain to students that the word *check* means to suddenly stop the forward progress of something or someone. Ask students to explain why we use the term *checks and balances* to describe our system of separation of powers.

Teacher Tip

Students may need help thinking of a graphic organizer or flowchart that illustrates a sequence of events. Draw a couple of examples for students to see.

SUPPORTING ADVANCED/GIFTED AND TALENTED INSTRUCTION

Expanding Information (45 minutes)

Researching Constitutional Amendments Have each student select one of the 27 amendments to the Constitution. Each student should use the library, Internet, or other sources to conduct research on the amendment he or she selected. Have students prepare a short paper explaining the history behind the amendment, arguments for and against the amendment, and the dates on which each state ratified the amendment. If time permits, have students present their findings to the class.

Section 3: Applying the Constitution

SUPPORTING ENGLISH-LANGUAGE INSTRUCTION

Analyzing Information (30 minutes)

Strict versus Loose Construction Review with the class the information from the section that refers to strict construction and loose construction of the Constitution. Remind students that strict construction means giving the words of the Constitution a literal meaning. Loose instruction means following the words of the Constitution, plus any reasonable inferences that can be drawn from them. Using the Constitution from the back of the textbook, select several passages from the Constitution and call on students to read them aloud. Then have the class explain the meaning of each passage. Finally, ask students to give examples of both strict and loose interpretations of each passage.

Vocabulary Tip
Point out to students that the term *construction* can also mean the act of interpreting or explaining something.

Section 1: Dividing Government Power

SUPPORTING ENGLISH-LANGUAGE INSTRUCTION

Applying Information (25 minutes)

Comparing Confederal and Federal Systems Discuss with students the chart in this section that compares a confederation to a federal system. Ask students to explain the difference between the two systems. Ask students to list the benefits and drawbacks of each system. Take notes on students' responses for everyone to see. Organize the class into pairs. Have one partner support a confederal system and the other support a federal system. Have students write a letter in which they attempt to persuade their partner that their assigned system is better. Encourage volunteers to share their letters with the class.

SUPPORTING SPECIAL EDUCATION INSTRUCTION

Analyzing Information (20 minutes)

Examining the Division of Government Power Have students use their own sheet of paper to copy the graphic organizer at right. Then have students reread the section, looking for powers exclusive to the national government or the state governments and for powers shared by both. Have students complete the graphic organizer as they read. When students are finished, have them discuss their answers with the class. Take notes on students' answers for everyone to see.

Section 2: American Federalism: Conflict and Change

SUPPORTING SPECIAL EDUCATION INSTRUCTION

Connecting Information (30 minutes)

Examining the Eras of Federalism Organize the class into eight small groups. Assign each group one of the following time periods: early Republic, pre–Civil War, Civil War, Reconstruction, turn-of-the-century, New Deal, Great Society, Reagan years. Have each group write a description of the relationship between state and national governments during its assigned era. Each group should identify two or three events that serve as examples of that relationship. For example, for the New Deal students might use the creation of

Resources

- Spanish Chapter Summaries Audio CD Program
- Differentiated Instruction Modified Worksheets and Tests on the Teacher One Stop™
  - Vocabulary Flash Cards
  - Vocabulary Activities
  - Chapter Review
  - Section Quizzes
  - Chapter Test
- Advanced Placement Review and Activities

Graphic Organizer

Dividing Government Power

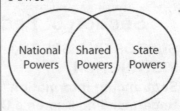

Teacher Tip

After students have completed their time lines, have them create a line graph that shows the shifts in the power of the national government. The graph will help students to visualize the changing nature of federalism.

national welfare programs as an example of the expansion of national power. Then reorganize the class into new groups that have one member representing each time period. Have the new groups create a time line that shows the changing relationship between the states and the national government. Display the completed time lines where students can see them.

SUPPORTING ADVANCED/GIFTED AND TALENTED INSTRUCTION

Expanding Information (30 minutes)

Investigating Eras of Federalism Ask students to identify the four eras of federalism. Students should list dual federalism, cooperative federalism, creative federalism, and new federalism. Organize students into four groups, one for each era of federalism. Have students use the library, Internet, or other sources to research information on the relationship between state governments and the national government during their assigned period. Then have each group cite at least three examples of this relationship. Have each group present its findings to the class. Have students take notes on each presentation in a graphic organizer like the one at right.

Graphic Organizer
The Eras of Federalism

Era	Examples
Dual federalism	

Section 3: Federalism Today

SUPPORTING SPECIAL EDUCATION INSTRUCTION

Sequencing Information (20 minutes)

Understanding Supreme Court Procedures Have students read the text under the heading "Supreme Court Procedures." Organize the class into small groups. Have each group make a list of the steps involved in a typical Supreme Court case. Then have each group create a diagram or flowchart that illustrates the processes and procedures involved in reaching a decision. Encourage students to share their diagrams with the class.

SUPPORTING ENGLISH-LANGUAGE INSTRUCTION

Expanding Information (45 minutes)

Writing Biographies Have students identify the current U.S. Supreme Court justices. Have each student select one Supreme Court Justice and conduct research on him or her. Have students write a short biography on the justice they selected. Remind students to include personal as well as professional information about their subject. Have volunteers share their biographies with the class.

Teacher Tip

If students have difficulty creating their own diagram, have them use a flowchart like the one below.

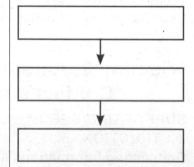

Lesson Plans for Differentiated Instruction

Section 1: Congress

SUPPORTING ENGLISH-LANGUAGE INSTRUCTION

Expanding Information (30 minutes)

Researching Your Representatives Have students read the text under the heading "Congress and the People." Lead a class discussion regarding the qualifications and characteristics of members of Congress. Ask students to identify characteristics they would want to see in their congressional representatives. Then have students research their current congressional representatives. Have students use the library, Internet, or other sources to gather information on their representatives' backgrounds, length of service, and committee assignments. Ask volunteers to present their research findings to the class. Then have students evaluate each representative's qualifications.

SUPPORTING SPECIAL EDUCATION INSTRUCTION

Summarizing Information (30 minutes)

Identifying Checks and Balances Have students read the text under the heading "Congress and Checks and Balances." Then have students use their own paper to create a graphic organizer like the one at right. Have students complete the graphic organizer by identifying the checks and balances that Congress has over the other two branches of the national government. Encourage volunteers to share their graphic organizers with the class.

Section 2: The Powers of Congress

SUPPORTING ADVANCED/GIFTED AND TALENTED INSTRUCTION

Expanding Information (40 minutes)

Examining the Powers of Congress After students have read the section, lead a class discussion on the powers of Congress. Ask students to identify some of the expressed and implied powers of Congress. Have students use the Internet to identify one recent piece of legislation. Instruct each student to write a short summary of the bill he or she selected. Then have students identify which expressed or implied power of Congress the bill reflects. Have students present their summaries to the class.

Resources

- Spanish Chapter Summaries Audio CD Program
- Differentiated Instruction Modified Worksheets and Tests on the Teacher One Stop™
  - Vocabulary Flash Cards
  - Vocabulary Activities
  - Chapter Review
  - Section Quizzes
  - Chapter Test
- Advanced Placement Review and Activities

Graphic Organizer

Congressional Checks and Balances

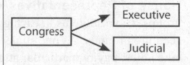

Teacher Tip

Students can use THOMAS, a Library of Congress Web site dedicated to legislative information, to research bills and laws. Visit THOMAS at http://thomas.loc.gov/.

SUPPORTING SPECIAL EDUCATION INSTRUCTION

Analyzing Information (30 minutes)

Understanding the Limits on Congress Have students reread the text under the heading "Limits on the Powers of Congress." Ask students to identify the various limits that have been imposed on Congress. Make a list of students' responses. Organize the class into pairs and assign each pair a specific limit on the power of Congress. Have each pair work together to write a letter to the editor. Letters should explain the assigned limit and provide several arguments in support of that limit. Ask volunteers to share their letters with the class.

Section 3: The House of Representatives

SUPPORTING ENGLISH-LANGUAGE INSTRUCTION

Summarizing Information (30 minutes)

House of Representatives Organize students into small groups. Have students in each group take turns reading this section in rounds. As one student reads aloud, have the others take notes, paying particular attention to names and new vocabulary trems. When the group is finished reading, have the students compare notes, filling in any gaps they may have. Then have students work as a group to write a summary of the entire section. Encourage students to read their summaries to the class.

SUPPORTING SPECIAL EDUCATION INSTRUCTION

Expanding Information (30 minutes)

Examining House Committees Organize the class into pairs. Then have each pair select two House committees from the chart titled "House Standing Committees." Instruct students to use the library, Internet, or other sources to research their selected committees. Students should look for information about the committee, committee chairperson, subcommittees, and the committee's responsibilities. Have students compile information on their committees in a chart like the one at right. Ask for volunteers to share their information with the class.

Teacher Tip

Remind students to keep their letters short and concise and to provide specific examples that support their arguments.

Graphic Organizer

House Committees

Committee		
Chairperson		
Responsibilities		
Subcommittees		

Section 4: The Senate

SUPPORTING ENGLISH-LANGUAGE INSTRUCTION
Comparing Information (30 minutes)
Understanding the Differences between the House and the Senate After students have read the section, have them contrast the House of Representatives with the Senate by completing a graphic organizer like the one at right. Students should review the section, looking for differences between the House of Representatives and the Senate, and should take notes in the graphic organizer. Remind students to consider factors such as qualifications for members, terms of office, structure, responsibilities, and powers. When students have finished their graphic organizers, lead a class discussion of the differences between the two houses of Congress. Ask students why the two houses are different.

Graphic Organizer
Differences between the House and Senate

House	Senate
two-year terms	six-year terms

Section 5: Congress at Work

SUPPORTING ADVANCED/GIFTED AND TALENTED INSTRUCTION
Synthesizing Information (45 minutes)
Conducting a Congressional Simulation Have students read and take notes on the section. Lead a class discussion in which you ask students to identify the various steps involved in the process of passing a bill. Then conduct a simulation in which students will introduce, debate, and vote on legislation. Start by organizing the class into two groups—one for the House of Representatives and one for the Senate. Organize the two large groups into several smaller groups and have each small group select a standing committee based on the interests of its members. Instruct each small group to author one piece of legislation on a relevant policy issue. Then have the two large groups introduce their bills and follow the legislative process: assign bills to committees, debate the bills in committee and on the floor, amend bills, and vote on bills. If time permits, have the two large groups exchange legislation once it is approved.

Teacher Tip
To facilitate the simulation, you may wish to have students elect a Speaker of the House and majority leader of the Senate. These individuals will assign bills to committees and assign members to the conference committee.

Section 1: The President

SUPPORTING ENGLISH-LANGUAGE INSTRUCTION

Visualizing Information (30 minutes)

Identifying the Roles of the President Have students read the text under the heading "Roles of the President." Then have each student make a list of the different roles the president serves. Remind students that the president serves in official roles outlined by the Constitution as well as in unofficial roles. Have students discuss responsibilities of the president in each role. Check to be sure that students understand the meaning of each role. Then have students draw a sketch that illustrates each role. Ask for volunteers to share their illustrations with the class.

SUPPORTING ADVANCED/GIFTED AND TALENTED INSTRUCTION

Expanding Information (45 minutes)

Debating the Electoral System After students have read the text under the heading "Election to Office," lead a class discussion on the role of the electoral college. Ask students to identify the two ways in which electors cast their votes. Organize the class into small groups and instruct half the students in each group to research the "winner-take-all" rule. Instruct the other half of students in each group to research the method of allocating votes used by Maine and Nebraska. After students have completed their research, have each group debate the merits of each system. Ask each group to reach a consensus on which method they prefer. Have volunteers from each group explain their rationale to the rest of the class.

Section 2: The Powers of the Presidency

SUPPORTING SPECIAL EDUCATION INSTRUCTION

Categorizing Information (30 minutes)

Identifying Presidential Powers After students have read the section, review with them the various powers of the president. Remind students that the president has executive, diplomatic, military, legislative, judicial, and informal powers. Have students complete a graphic organizer like the one at right, using specific examples for each type of power. You may want to have students share their examples with the class.

Resources

- Spanish Chapter Summaries Audio CD Program

- Differentiated Instruction Modified Worksheets and Tests on the Teacher One Stop™
  - Vocabulary Flash Cards
  - Vocabulary Activities
  - Chapter Review
  - Section Quizzes
  - Chapter Test

- Advanced Placement Review and Activities

Teacher Tip

Have students identify the official roles of the president by locating the wording in the Constitution that outlines each role.

Teacher Tip

Have students conduct research on ideas for reforming the electoral college system. Encourage students to share their findings with the class.

Graphic Organizer

Powers of the President

Powers	Examples
Executive	
Diplomatic	
Military	
Legislative	
Judicial	
Informal	

SUPPORTING ADVANCED/GIFTED AND TALENTED INSTRUCTION
Connecting Information (45 minutes)
Creating a Time Line After students have read the text under the heading "Changes in Presidential Power," discuss with the class the ways in which presidential power has expanded over time. Have students use the library, Internet, and other sources to research this expansion of presidential power. Then have students create a time line that illustrates the changes in presidential power. Encourage students to share their time lines with the class.

Teacher Tip
Have students examine the time line in this section titled "Growth of Presidential Power" before they begin work on their own time line.

Section 3: The President's Administration

SUPPORTING SPECIAL EDUCATION INSTRUCTION
Evaluating Information (30 minutes)
Understanding the President's Administration After students have read the section, have them create a graphic organizer to identify the various roles of the president's administration. Working with a partner, students should identify the various members and responsibilities of each group. As an extension activity, you may want to have students conduct research to identify some of the current members of the president's staff.

Graphic Organizer
Key Roles in the President's Administration

SUPPORTING ENGLISH-LANGUAGE INSTRUCTION
Expanding Information (45 minutes)
Examining the Cabinet Have students read the text under the heading "The Cabinet." Organize the class into pairs. Then have each pair use the library, Internet, or other sources to research the history of the president's cabinet, beginning with the first cabinet. Have each pair take notes on the changes that have taken place over the years. Then have each pair create a time line that illustrates these changes and identifies the additions of new executive departments. Have each pair present its time line to the class.

Section 1: The Federal Bureaucracy

SUPPORTING ADVANCED/GIFTED AND TALENTED INSTRUCTION

Expanding Information (30 minutes)

Researching the Federal Bureaucracy Lead a class discussion on the size of the federal bureaucracy. Point out to students that the federal government is the nation's largest employer, employing almost 3 million people. Have students conduct research on the types of jobs available in the federal bureaucracy. Have students use the library, Internet, or other sources to search for information about the different jobs within the federal bureaucracy. Ask students to keep a list of the jobs they find. Then have students compile a class list.

SUPPORTING SPECIAL EDUCATION INSTRUCTION

Contrasting Information (20 minutes)

Examining the Civil Service Have students read the text under the heading "The Civil Service." Discuss with the class the spoils system that was used early in the nation's history. Have students create a graphic organizer like the one at right. Then have students list the characteristics of each system—the spoils system and the modern civil service system. When students are finished, have them write a brief description of how these two systems differ.

Section 2: Executive Departments and Independent Agencies

SUPPORTING SPECIAL EDUCATION INSTRUCTION

Researching Information (45 minutes)

Examining Executive Departments Assign each student 1 of the 15 executive branch departments. Have students use the library, Internet, or other sources to research information about their assigned departments. Students should take notes on the key responsibilities of their assigned department, important agencies within their department, and current leaders of the department. Have each student create a graphic organizer like the one at right. Students should use information from their research notes to complete the graphic organizer. Encourage volunteers to share their findings with the class.

Resources

- Spanish Chapter Summaries Audio CD Program

- Differentiated Instruction Modified Worksheets and Tests on the Teacher One Stop™
  – Vocabulary Flash Cards
  – Vocabulary Activities
  – Chapter Review
  – Section Quizzes
  – Chapter Test

- Advanced Placement Review and Activities

Graphic Organizer
Examining the Civil Service

Spoils System	Civil Service System

Graphic Organizer
Executive Departments

Teacher Tip

Students might want to visit http://www.usa.gov/ for an overview of each executive branch department.

SUPPORTING ENGLISH-LANGUAGE INSTRUCTION

Analyzing Information (30 minutes)

Examining Independent Agencies Have students take notes as they read the text under the heading "Independent Agencies." Instruct students to use a chart like the one at right to take notes on the different types of independent agencies. Have students start by labeling each column with one of the three types of agencies. For each type of independent agency, students should copy the definition from the textbook and then write a description in their own words. Finally, students should list several examples of each type of independent agency in the chart.

Graphic Organizer

Independent Agencies

Definition			
Description			
Examples			

Section 3: Financing Government

SUPPORTING ADVANCED/GIFTED AND TALENTED INSTRUCTION

Expanding Information (45 minutes)

Illustrating the Federal Budget Have students research the federal budget for the current fiscal year. Instruct students to use the library, Internet, or other sources to find the amounts budgeted for each major department or agency. Then have students compile their findings in either a bar graph or a pie chart. Encourage students to share their completed graphs with the class.

Teacher Tip

Have students begin their research by visiting the federal government's Web page on the budget at http://www.gpoaccess.gov/usbudget.

SUPPORTING SPECIAL EDUCATION INSTRUCTION

Connecting Information (45 minutes)

Debating the Budget Discuss with students the steps in the budget process. Organize the class into groups and assign each group one of the following roles: president, Office of Management and Budget, federal departments and agencies, House Budget Committee, Senate Budget Committee, and conference committee. Discuss with the class the role each group plays in determining the federal budget. Have students conduct a simulation of the budget process. The group representing federal departments and agencies will request annual budgets. Then the president and Office of Management and Budget groups will work together to create a proposed budget. Their budget passes on to the budget committees, who each debate and vote on the proposed budget. The conference committee negotiates any differences between the two versions, and the president approves the budget.

Teacher Tip

Have students take notes on the steps involved in the budget process in a diagram like the one below.

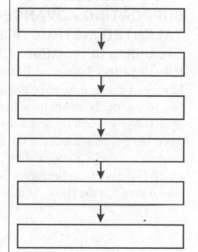

Section 1: The Federal Court System

SUPPORTING SPECIAL EDUCATION INSTRUCTION

Organizing Information (20 minutes)

Understanding the Federal Court System After students have read the text under the heading "Structure of the Federal Court System," have them examine the chart titled "The Federal Court System." Discuss with students the general structure of the U.S. courts. Have students work in pairs to create a graphic organizer or illustration that explains the hierarchy of the federal court system. Ask volunteers to share their diagrams with the class.

SUPPORTING ENGLISH-LANGUAGE INSTRUCTION

Interpreting Information (30 minutes)

Understanding Vocabulary Before students read the section, help them learn the key terms they will encounter. Start by writing the key terms for students to see. Have students copy the terms in a chart like the one at right. Using the glossary in the back of the textbook, students should write down the definition for each key term. Then go over each term with the class, explaining the meaning of each term in language the students can understand. Finally, have students complete the chart by writing down the meaning of each term in their own words.

Section 2: Lower Federal Courts

SUPPORTING ADVANCED/GIFTED AND TALENTED INSTRUCTION

Expanding Information (40 minutes)

Investigating Types of Federal Courts After students have read the section, have them discuss the various types of federal courts. Have students list each of the different federal courts. Assign each student a different court from the list. Then have each student use the library, Internet, or other sources to research information about his or her assigned court. Have students prepare a 5- to 10-minute presentation in which they tell the class about their research findings.

Resources

- Spanish Chapter Summaries Audio CD Program
- Differentiated Instruction Modified Worksheets and Tests on the Teacher One Stop™
  - Vocabulary Flash Cards
  - Vocabulary Activities
  - Chapter Review
  - Section Quizzes
  - Chapter Test
- Advanced Placement Review and Activities

Graphic Organizer
Key Terms

Term	Definition	Meaning
jurisdiction		

Teacher Tip

Recommend that students begin their research by visiting the federal government's Web site on the federal judiciary at www.uscourts.gov/.

SUPPORTING SPECIAL EDUCATION INSTRUCTION

Analyzing Information (20 minutes)
Comparing U.S. District Courts and Courts of Appeals Have students read the text under the headings "Federal District Courts" and "Federal Courts of Appeals." Then have students draw a Venn diagram similar to the one at right. Have students complete the diagram by identifying the similarities and differences between the federal district courts and the federal courts of appeals.

Graphic Organizer

U.S. District Courts and Courts of Appeals

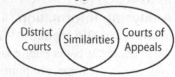

Section 3: The Supreme Court

SUPPORTING SPECIAL EDUCATION INSTRUCTION

Sequencing Information (20 minutes)
Understanding Supreme Court Procedures Have students read the text under the heading "Supreme Court Procedures." Organize the class into small groups. Have each group make a list of the steps involved in a typical Supreme Court case. Then have each group create a diagram or flowchart that illustrates the processes and procedures involved in reaching a decision. Encourage students to share their diagrams with the class.

Teacher Tip
If students have difficulty creating their own diagram, have them use a flowchart like the one below.

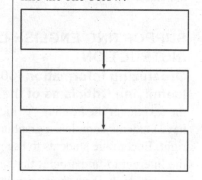

SUPPORTING ADVANCED/GIFTED AND TALENTED INSTRUCTION

Expanding Information (45 minutes)
Writing Biographies Have students identify the current U.S. Supreme Court justices. Instruct each student to select one Supreme Court justice and to conduct research on him or her. Have students write a short biography on the justice they selected. Remind students to include personal as well as professional information about their subject. Have volunteers share their biographies with the class.

Section 1: Public Opinion

SUPPORTING SPECIAL EDUCATION INSTRUCTION

Analyzing Information (45 minutes)

Identifying Differences Have students read the text under the heading "What is Public Opinion?" Help students understand the impact of public opinion on public policy and the two different views of public opinion—one in which public opinion is a single, centralized body that may be led by public policy and the other in which the public consists of many individual opinions that help to shape public policy. Then have students work in pairs to identify a specific example that illustrates each view of public opinion. Encourage students to use the examples in the textbook as a starting point. Ask for volunteers to share their examples with the class.

SUPPORTING ENGLISH-LANGUAGE INSTRUCTION

Organizing Information (30 minutes)

Identifying Criticisms of the Media Have students read the text under the heading "Criticism of the Media." Then have students complete a graphic organizer like the one at right. Encourage students to use newspapers, magazines, and the Internet to find articles that reflect each type of criticism. Have students share their completed graphic organizers with the rest of the class.

Section 2: Interest Groups

SUPPORTING ADVANCED/GIFTED AND TALENTED INSTRUCTION

Expanding Information (40 minutes)

Types of Interest Groups Discuss with the class the different types of interest groups mentioned in the section. Have students select a specific type of interest group to research. Then have students create a fictional interest group that meets the characteristics of they type they selected. Have students develop a plan of action for their fictional interest group, including identifying the types of candidates their group might support, how their group might inform public opinion, and what officials their group would need to lobby to pursue their agenda. Encourage students to share their information with the rest of the class.

Resources

- Spanish Chapter Summaries Audio CD Program
- Differentiated Instruction Modified Worksheets and Tests on the Teacher's One Stop™
  – Vocabulary Flash Cards
  – Vocabulary Activities
  – Chapter Review
  – Section Quizzes
  – Chapter Test
- Advanced Placement Review and Activities

Graphic Organizer
Criticism of the Media

Criticism	Examples
Reporting Bias	
Story Selection Bias	
Factual Inaccuracy	
Media Consolidation	

Teacher Tip
Have students conduct research of actual interest groups for examples of real-life issues, actions, and policies.

SUPPORTING SPECIAL EDUCATION INSTRUCTION

Applying Information (30 minutes)

Examining Interest Groups Have students reread the text under the heading "How Interest Groups Work." As you discuss the actions of interest groups with the class, have students develop a list of activities in which interest groups engage. Then organize students into small groups. Assign each group a specific interest group mentioned in the section. Have each group develop a list of goals they want to accomplish. For example, Mothers Against Drunk Driving may want to pass legislation calling for stricter penalties for repeat offenders. Then have the groups identify activities discussed in the section that would help them accomplish each goal. Have students share their goals and activities with the rest of the class.

Graphic Organizer

Goals and Activities of Interest Groups

Goals	Activities

Section 3: Political Parties

SUPPORTING SPECIAL EDUCATION INSTRUCTION

Evaluating Information (30 minutes)

Benefits and Criticisms of Political Parties Have students reread the text under the heading "Political Parties and the Public Good." Have students to work in pairs to answer the following question: *Are political parties a benefit to the American political system?* Have students start by completing a graphic organizer like the one at right. Then have each pair agree on an answer to the question. Have each pair make a list of the reasons why they answered as they did.

Graphic Organizer

Evaluating the Role of American Political Parties

Benefits	Criticisms

SUPPORTING ADVANCED/GIFTED AND TALENTED INSTRUCTION

Expanding Information (45 minutes)

Researching Political Parties Have students examine the time line titled "American Political Parties." Have each student select a political party from the time line. Instruct students to use the library, Internet, or other sources to research their selected political party. Students should focus their research on the history of their political party, including important members of the party, key issues, and campaign successes and failures. Encourage students to share their findings with the class.

Teacher Tip

Have each student create and present a five-slide multimedia presentation that highlights the issues and history of their selected political party.

Section 4: The Electoral Process

SUPPORTING ENGLISH-LANGUAGE INSTRUCTION

Summarizing Information (30 minutes)

The Electoral Process Organize students into small groups. Have them take turns reading Section 4 in rounds. As one student reads aloud, have the others take notes, paying particular attention to names and new vocabulary. When the group is finished reading, have the students compare notes, filling in any gaps they may have. Then have each group create a summary of the section.

Teacher Tip
Have students keep a list of vocabulary and other terms with which they are not familiar. Have students define each term in their own words.

SUPPORTING ADVANCED/GIFTED AND TALENTED INSTRUCTION

Synthesizing information (45 minutes)

Holding an Election Have students stage a mock class election. Call on volunteers to play the role of candidates. Have the other students play the role of voters. Start by asking the voters to create a list of key issues. Then have the candidates create political campaigns and state their stance on each of the issues. Allow the voters an opportunity to question the candidates. Then have students vote by secret ballot. Following the vote, ask students to discuss why they voted the way they did.

Teacher Tip
Assign students different tasks in the class election. For example, some students might be in charge of staging the election, while others might help work on campaigns or register students to vote in the election.

Section 1: Protecting Constitutional Rights

SUPPORTING ENGLISH-LANGUAGE INSTRUCTION

Understanding Information (20 minutes)

Understanding Civil Liberties and Civil Rights Have students reread the text under the heading "The Ten Amendments." Discuss with students the difference between the terms *civil liberties* and *civil rights*. Explain to students that civil liberties are protections that individuals have from government interference with their basic freedoms, such as freedom of speech and freedom of religion. Civil rights are guarantees that citizens have for fair and equal application of their rights as citizens, such as the right to vote. Instruct each student to draw two illustrations, one depicting the meaning of civil liberties and one depicting the meaning of civil rights. Encourage students to share their illustrations with the rest of the class.

SUPPORTING SPECIAL EDUCATION INSTRUCTION

Expanding Information (45 minutes)

Understanding the Doctrine of Incorporation Have students read the text under the heading "Civil Liberties and the Fourteenth Amendment." Help students understand the incorporation doctrine by explaining to them that the Supreme Court has, at various times, ruled that many of the protections provided in the amendments to the Constitution apply to the states as well as to the national government. For example, just as the national government must refrain from any establishment of an official religion, so must state governments. Have students read the chart titled "Process of Incorporation" and select a Supreme Court case from the chart. Instruct students to research their case and to complete a graphic organizer like the one at right. Students should write a short explanation of how their case affected the states.

Resources

- Spanish Chapter Summaries Audio CD Program
- Differentiated Instruction Modified Worksheets and Tests on the Teacher One Stop™
  - Vocabulary Flash Cards
  - Vocabulary Activities
  - Chapter Review
  - Section Quizzes
  - Chapter Test
- Advanced Placement Review and Activities

Teacher Tip

One Web site to recommend to students for their research is The Oyez Project at www.oyez.org/.

Graphic Organizer

Amendment	
Provision	
Supreme Court Decision	
Facts of the Case	

Section 2: First Amendment Freedoms

SUPPORTING SPECIAL EDUCATION INSTRUCTION

Organizing Information (30 minutes)

Understanding Limits on Freedoms Have students work in pairs to complete a graphic organizer like the one at right. Have students begin by examining the freedoms guaranteed in the First Amendment and entering those in the graphic organizer. Then have students skim the section to look for limits on each freedom.

SUPPORTING ADVANCED/GIFTED AND TALENTED INSTRUCTION

Evaluating Information (45 minutes)

Debating the Issue Have students read the text under the heading "Symbolic Speech." Then discuss with the class the controversy surrounding the issue of flag burning. Stage a class debate focused on the following proposition: *Americans should support a constitutional amendment outlawing the burning of the American flag.* Organize students into two groups—one in favor of the proposition and one against. Have students use the library, Internet, or other sources to research the topic of flag burning. Then have each group debate one another. Close the debate by asking students on which side of the debate they stand.

Section 3: Protecting Individual Liberties

SUPPORTING ENGLISH-LANGUAGE INSTRUCTION

Interpreting Information (30 minutes)

Understanding Vocabulary Terms Write the following terms for students to see: *right to bear arms*, *quartering of soldiers*, *probable cause*, *search and seizure*, *exclusionary rule*, *surveillance*, *wiretapping*, *procedural due process*, and *substantive due process*. Organize students into small groups and assign each group a term from the list. Have groups use dictionaries, the textbook, and other sources to help define their term. Then have each group explain its term to the class. Instruct students to take notes on each group's explanation in a chart like the one at right.

Graphic Organizer

First Amendment Freedoms and Limits

Freedoms	→	Limits
	→	
	→	
	→	
	→	

Teacher Tip

Have students start their research by examining efforts to pass a flag desecration amendment.

Teacher Tip

Remind students that facts and statistics are good tools to help support their stance.

Graphic Organizer

Vocabulary Terms

Term	Definition

SUPPORTING SPECIAL EDUCATION INSTRUCTION
Expanding Information (45 minutes)
Examining Protections for Students Have students reread the text under the heading "Protections for Students." Organize the class into pairs and assign the groups to one of the following Supreme Court cases: *New Jersey* v. *T.L.O.*, *Vernonia School District* v. *Acton*, *Board of Education of Pottawatomie County* v. *Earls*. Have each pair research its assigned case using the library, Internet, or other sources. Have each pair write a short summary of its case and the Court's decision. Then have each pair present its findings to the class. Have students take notes on each presentation.

Teacher Tip
You may want to have students research cases other than those mentioned in this section. Other cases relating to protections for students include *Tinker* v. *Des Moines*, *Bethel School District* v. *Fraser*, *Hazelwood School District* v. *Kuhlmeier*, *Morse* v. *Frederick*, and *Goss* v. *Lopez*.

Section 4: Crime and Punishment
SUPPORTING ENGLISH-LANGUAGE INSTRUCTION
Sequencing Information (30 minutes)
Examining Criminal Case Processes Have students reread the text under the heading "Criminal Case Processes." Then have each student list the different steps involved in a criminal case. Instruct each student to create a time line or flowchart depicting the sequence of events. If time permits, have students illustrate their time lines with images that symbolize each stage in the process. Encourage students to share their time lines with the rest of the class.

Teacher Tip
Have students keep a list of vocabulary and other unfamiliar terms from the section. Have students define each term in their own words.

SUPPORTING ADVANCED/GIFTED AND TALENTED INSTRUCTION
Synthesizing Information (45 minutes)
Arguing a Supreme Court Case Have students stage a mock Supreme Court trial on the issue of cruel and unusual punishments. Have students start by researching the rules and procedures of a Supreme Court trial. Then have students work together to create a hypothetical case that has been appealed to the U.S. Supreme Court. Assign students various roles in the trial. Roles include nine Supreme Court justices, several attorneys for each party, the clerk of the Supreme Court, the marshal, marshal's aides, and special guests. Have each student conduct research into the role he or she will play and into the topic of cruel and unusual punishments. Have students stage the mock trial using the guidelines of the Supreme Court. At the end of oral arguments, allow the Supreme Court justices a few minutes to deliberate and issue an oral opinion.

Teacher Tip
Encourage students to review the Court Rules and Visitors' Guide to Argument found on the Supreme Court Web site at www.supremecourtus.gov/ for help preparing the mock Supreme Court trial.

Section 1: Civil Rights and Discrimination

SUPPORTING SPECIAL EDUCATION INSTRUCTION

Expanding Information (45 minutes)

Researching Discrimination Have students read the text under the heading "A Pattern of Discrimination." Lead a class discussion of the history of discrimination that certain groups have faced. Point out to students that at various times in the history of the United States, certain types of discrimination were legal. Organize the class into five groups. Assign each group one of the groups of Americans discussed in the reading. Have students use the library, Internet, or other sources to research specific instances in which a member of their assigned group of Americans was subject to legal discrimination. Then have students research laws or judicial decisions in which some form of discrimination against that group was outlawed. Have each group present their findings to the class.

SUPPORTING ENGLISH-LANGUAGE INSTRUCTION

Organizing Information (30 minutes)

Identifying Changes in Civil Rights Discuss with students the key civil rights covered in the section. Remind students that civil rights deal with fairness and equal treatment but that not every group in the United States has always experienced fair and equal treatment. Ask each student to identify three racial, ethnic, or other groups that have experienced unfair treatment at some point in U.S. history. Have students cite examples of the difficulties each group faced. Ask students to compile their findings in a graphic organizer like the one at right. Then have students identify how civil rights protections for each group have changed over time. Ask for volunteers to share their graphic organizers with the class.

Resources

- Spanish Chapter Summaries Audio CD Program
- Differentiated Instruction Modified Worksheets and Tests on the Teacher One Stop™
  - Vocabulary Flash Cards
  - Vocabulary Activities
  - Chapter Review
  - Section Quizzes
  - Chapter Test
- Advanced Placement Review and Activities

Graphic Organizer

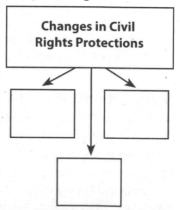

Changes in Civil Rights Protections

Section 2: Equal Justice under Law

SUPPORTING ADVANCED/GIFTED AND TALENTED INSTRUCTION

Analyzing Information (30 minutes)

Examining Equal Protection Have students read the text under the heading "Equal Protection of the Law." Then discuss with the class the equal protection clause of the Fourteenth Amendment and the different tests that courts use to determine if reasonable distinction exists. Before beginning the activity, develop a list of scenarios that may or may not violate the equal protection clause, for example a national women's rights group denying membership to males. Write each scenario on a slip of paper. Then have each student randomly draw a scenario. Have students determine if reasonable distinction exists or if the scenario is a violation of the equal protection clause. Ask students to identify which of the three key tests—rational basis, intermediate scrutiny, or strict scrutiny—would best apply to their scenario. Encourage students to explain their scenario and decision to the class.

Teacher Tip

Have students examine the feature titled "Applying Equal Protection" for an example of a specific scenario. You may choose to have students use the feature as an example of how students can write their own scenario and decision.

SUPPORTING ENGLISH LANGUAGE INSTRUCTION

Understanding Information (20 minutes)

Examining Segregation Have students read the text under the heading "Rolling Back Segregation." To help students understand the terms *de jure segregation* and *de facto segregation*, have students create a graphic organizer like the one at right. Have students write a definition of each term in the boxes on the left. Then have students list examples of each type of segregation on the right. After students have finished, have them share their answers with the class.

Graphic Organizer
Understanding Segregation

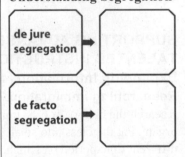

Section 3: Civil Rights Laws

SUPPORTING SPECIAL EDUCATION INSTRUCTION

Organizing Information (30 minutes)

Creating a Civil Rights Time Line As students read the section, have them keep a list of major legislation and rulings that helped expand civil rights protections in the United States. Have students create a time line of the events they noted. Remind students to place their events in chronological order and to list the year in which the event took place.

Graphic Organizer
Extending Civil Rights

SUPPORTING ENGLISH LANGUAGE INSTRUCTION

Evaluating Information (45 minutes)

Debating Affirmative Action Have students read the Debating the Issue feature on affirmative action. Organize the class into small groups. Assign each group one of the viewpoints on affirmative action—government should support affirmative action policies, or government should not support them. Have each group use the library, Internet, or other sources to research arguments that support its stance. Have each group give a brief presentation persuading the class to agree with its viewpoint.

Teacher Tip

After each group has made its presentation, discuss with the class which arguments were most persuasive and why.

Section 4: Citizenship and Immigration

SUPPORTING SPECIAL EDUCATION INSTRUCTION

Summarizing Information (20 minutes)

Have students read the text under the heading "U.S. Citizenship." Discuss with the class the ways a person can gain citizenship in the United States. Then have students complete a graphic organizer, like the one at right, in which they summarize the three methods of gaining citizenship. Ask volunteers to share their graphic organizers with the class.

Graphic Organizer
U.S. Citizenship

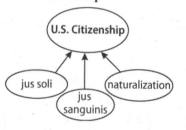

SUPPORTING ADVANCED/GIFTED AND TALENTED INSTRUCTION

Expanding Information (45 minutes)

Researching Immigration Policy Ask students to research the history of U.S. immigration policy. Start by organizing the class into small groups. Assign each group a different time period on which to focus its research. Have students use the library, Internet, or other sources to find information about U.S. immigration policies during their assigned historical period. Have each group identify legislation that impacted immigration policy as well as public reaction to those policies. Then have each group prepare a short multimedia presentation that showcases its findings. If time permits, have each group present its multimedia presentation to the class.

Teacher Tip

Suggest that students visit the U.S. Citizenship and Immigration Services Web site at http://www.uscis.gov for information on current immigration policies. Students may also want to examine the Congressional Budget Office's special collection on immigration policy at http://cbo.gov/publications.

Section 1: Election Campaigns

SUPPORTING ENGLISH-LANGUAGE INSTRUCTION

Prereading (10 minutes)

Preparing an Outline Have students preview the section by using the main headings and subheadings to prepare an outline structure. Have students look for other important information, such as key terms or captions, that they can anticipate including as subtopics or supporting details. For example, the chart titled "The Campaign Team" should indicate to students an important subtopic to include in their outlines. Remind students that they are only preparing the outline structure. They will fill in the outline in the next step.

Reading (30 minutes)

Creating an Outline Using the outline structure they prepared as part of the prereading stage, students should now read the section and complete the outline. You may want to have students work in pairs to fill in their outlines. As students read the section, have them fill in the outline with key information about election campaigns. Remind students that an outline contains the main ideas and any supporting details. Supporting details should be indented to show their relationship to the main ideas.

Section 2: Campaign Funding and Political Action Committees

SUPPORTING SPECIAL EDUCATION INSTRUCTION

Summarizing Information (30 minutes)

Understanding Campaign Funding Have students read the text under the heading "Funding Election Campaigns." Lead a class discussion about the sources of campaign funding. Have students use a graphic organizer like the one at right to take notes on the discussion. Ask students why the various sources of campaign funding might pose problems. Ask students to identify the steps the government has taken to regulate campaign funding. Has regulation been successful? Why or why not?

Resources

- Spanish Chapter Summaries Audio CD Program
- Differentiated Instruction Modified Worksheets and Tests on the Teacher One Stop™
  – Vocabulary Flash Cards
  – Vocabulary Activities
  – Chapter Review
  – Section Quizzes
  – Chapter Test
- Advanced Placement Review and Activities

Teacher Tip

A number of newspapers and magazines track election campaigns. Encourage students to learn more about upcoming elections by visiting Web sites of local newspapers as well as Internet news sites.

Graphic Organizer

Sources of Campaign Funds

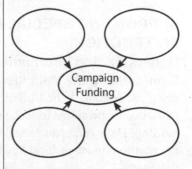

Teacher Tip

Have students examine campaign funding reports available from the Federal Election Commission's Web site at www.fec.gov.

SUPPORTING ADVANCED/GIFTED AND TALENTED INSTRUCTION

Expanding Information (45 minutes)

Researching Interest Groups Have students read the text under the heading "Interest Groups and Election Campaigns." Have students discuss the types of interest groups mentioned in this section. Ask students to identify the similarities and differences between the different interest groups. Have students use the library, Internet, or other sources to find real-world examples of each of the different types of interest groups. Students should use a chart like the one at right to note their findings. If time permits, have students present their findings to the class.

Graphic Organizer
Interest Groups

	Name	Activities
PAC		
Leadership PAC		
527 Group		

Section 3: Election Day and the Voters

SUPPORTING ENGLISH-LANGUAGE INSTRUCTION

Sequencing Information (20 minutes)

Examining the Right to Vote Have students read the text under the heading "Voting Rights and Responsibilities." Then have each student make a time line depicting the expansion of voting rights in the United States. Ask students why they think voting rights were difficult for some groups to gain. Then ask students to determine if there are still groups in American society who should be granted the right to vote. Ask students to provide support for their answers.

SUPPORTING SPECIAL EDUCATION INSTRUCTION

Understanding Information (30 minutes)

Summarizing the Main Idea Have students read the text under the heading "The Voting Process." Then have students work in pairs to summarize the information under each sub-heading. Have each pair reread the section, summarizing the information under each subheading in two to three meaningful sentences.

Teacher Tip
If students have difficulty creating time lines, have them complete a graphic organizer like the one below.

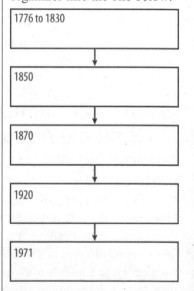

1776 to 1830

1850

1870

1920

1971

Section 1: The First Amendment: Your Freedom of Expression

SUPPORTING ADVANCED/GIFTED AND TALENTED INSTRUCTION

Expanding Information (45 minutes)

Debating Students' Right of Expression Start by having students reread the Case Study "Students' Right of Expression." Then organize the class into two groups—one in favor of limiting students' right of expression and one against limiting students' right of expression. Have students from each group work together in smaller groups to consider what kinds of arguments might be made both for and against their stance. Have students prepare their arguments for a class debate. Students should also prepare questions to pose to members of the opposing group during the debate. Stage a debate in which students debate the following proposition: *Students' right to free expression should be equal to that of adults.* Encourage all students to participate in the debate in some way—either as active participants or as an involved audience member. At the end of the debate, poll students to identify their personal opinions on the topic. Ask students if their opinions were swayed by the arguments made during the debate.

SUPPORTING ENGLISH-LANGUAGE INSTRUCTION

Expanding Information (30 minutes)

Identifying First Amendment Cases After students have read the section, discuss the key points with the class. Have students identify the various freedoms protected by the First Amendment. Then have each student draw a graphic organizer like the one at right on his or her own sheet of paper. Have students select a case mentioned in the text for each freedom guaranteed by the First Amendment. Then have students use the library, Internet, or other sources to find more information about each case they selected. Have students identify the outcome of each case and its influence on the rights of Americans. Encourage students to share their charts with the class.

Resources

- Spanish Chapter Summaries Audio CD Program
- Differentiated Instruction Modified Worksheets and Tests on the Teacher One Stop™
  - Vocabulary Flash Cards
  - Vocabulary Activities
  - Chapter Review
  - Section Quizzes
  - Chapter Test
- Advanced Placement Review and Activities

Teacher Tip

To help students prepare for the debate, you may want to have them fill in a chart like the one below.

Arguments For	Arguments Against	Questions

Graphic Organizer

First Amendment Cases

Freedom	Case	Outcome
Religion		
Speech		
Press		
Petition and Assembly		
Student Assembly		

Section 2: The Fourth Amendment: Your Right to Be Secure

SUPPORTING SPECIAL EDUCATION INSTRUCTION

Analyzing Information (45 minutes)

Evaluating a Fourth Amendment Decision Have students read the text under the heading "Students' Fourth Amendment Rights." Then discuss with the class the case *New Jersey* v. *T.L.O.* You may wish to have students read the summary of the case provided in the Supreme Court Case Decisions in their back of the textbook. Have students discuss the Supreme Court's decision. Then have each student write a short response in which they defend or oppose the Court's ruling. Remind students to provide support for their opinions.

Teacher Tip
Have students learn more about *New Jersey* v. *T.L.O.* by reading a summary of the case at The Oyez Project Web site at www.oyez.org/.

Section 3: Due Process and the Fourteenth Amendment

SUPPORTING ENGLISH-LANGUAGE INSTRUCTION

Analyzing Information (30 minutes)

Comparing Procedural and Substantive Due Process
Before students read the section, discuss the terms *procedural due process* and *substantive due process* with the class. Have students read the feature titled "Understanding Due Process." Explain to students that procedural due process is designed to guarantee that government procedures are applied fairly for all people. Substantive due process is designed to ensure that governments respect a person's rights and freedoms. Review the cases that serve as examples for each type of due process. Check to be sure that students understand the difference between procedural and substantive due process. Have students skim the section to look for examples of each type of due process. Then have students work in pairs to complete a graphic organizer like the one at right, placing the examples they found in the correct column.

Graphic Organizer
Understanding Due Process

Procedural	Substantive

Section 4: Federalism and the Supreme Court

SUPPORTING SPECIAL EDUCATION INSTRUCTION

Interpreting Information (30 minutes)

Creating Political Cartoons Have students read the text under the headings "The Guns in School Case" and "The Medical Marijuana Case." Discuss with the class students' opinions about the Court's rulings in each case. Do students agree or disagree with the Supreme Court? Have students defend their answers. Ask each student to select one case to be the subject of a political cartoon. Have students start by taking a stand on the Supreme Court's ruling. Students' political cartoons should reflect their opinions of the decision. Remind students that political cartoons express the artist's point of view or opinion and use symbols to express complex ideas. Encourage students to share their political cartoons with the rest of the class.

SUPPORTING ADVANCED/GIFTED AND TALENTED INSTRUCTION

Synthesizing Information (30 minutes)

Predicting Future Federalism Cases After students have read the section, have them refer back in their textbooks to Chapter 4: Federalism. Have students reread the portion of Section 3 titled "Issues in Federalism Today." Have students use the issues mentioned in Chapter 4 as well as other issues to predict future conflicts over the expansion of federal authority. Have the class make a list of possible conflicts. Discuss the possible conflicts with the class.

Teacher Tip

Encourage students to use the library, Internet, and other sources to research other Supreme Court cases relating to the expansion of national authority.

Teacher Tip

Before students begin working on their own political cartoons, encourage them to look through their textbooks or on the Internet for examples of political cartoons that express a point of view relating to Supreme Court decisions.

Section 1: Foreign Policy Choices in a Complex World

SUPPORTING ENGLISH-LANGUAGE INSTRUCTION

Understanding Information (45 minutes)

Examining Foreign Policy Goals Have students read the list titled "The Five Goals of Foreign Policy." Discuss with the class the meaning of each goal. Check to be sure that students understand each goal. Have students work in small groups to research news articles relating to American foreign policy. Students should find recent examples that illustrate each of the five goals. Have each group present its examples to the class. If time permits, have students perform the same activity with examples of the three ways in which the United States applies foreign policy.

SUPPORTING SPECIAL EDUCATION INSTRUCTION

Categorizing Information (30 minutes)

Understanding the Tools of Foreign Policy Start by asking students to reread the chart titled "Economic Sanctions." As you discuss the chart with the class, tell the students that they will answer the same questions for the other two tools of foreign policy—diplomacy and military. Have students draw a chart like the one at right on their own sheet of paper. For each tool of foreign policy, students should identify its purpose, types, and pros and cons. Have students start by filling in their charts with the information on economic tools. Point out to students that they already have this information completed for them in the chart in their textbook. Then have students work on their own to identify the definition, purpose, types, and pros and cons of the other two tools. You may wish to repeat the questions from the chart in the textbook to help students understand what information goes in each portion of the chart.

Resources

- Spanish Chapter Summaries Audio CD Program

- Differentiated Instruction Modified Worksheets and Tests on the Teacher One Stop™
  - Vocabulary Flash Cards
  - Vocabulary Activities
  - Chapter Review
  - Section Quizzes
  - Chapter Test

- Advanced Placement Review and Activities

Graphic Organizer

Tools of Foreign Policy

Diplomatic	Economic	Military

Section 2: How Domestic Actors Affect Foreign Policy

SUPPORTING SPECIAL EDUCATION INSTRUCTION

Expanding Information (45 minutes)
Researching Presidential Foreign Policy Powers
Have students reread the text under the heading "Executive Powers." Then assign each student to one of two topics—the president as diplomat or the president as commander in chief. Using the library, Internet, and other sources, students should conduct research to find at least five examples of occasions in which presidents have used their power as diplomat or commander in chief to achieve foreign policy goals. Have students create a time line of the events they found in their research. Have students write a short description for each event. Ask volunteers to share their time lines with the class.

SUPPORTING ADVANCED/GIFTED AND TALENTED INSTRUCTION

Applying Information (30 minutes)
Creating Foreign Policy Scenarios Have students read the text under the heading "The President, Congress, and Foreign Policy." Have each student write a brief description of a possible foreign policy situation that the United States could face. Then have students exchange their descriptions with a partner. Each student should use the information he or she learned about presidential and congressional roles in shaping foreign policy to develop an action plan dealing with his or her partner's foreign policy scenario. Have students complete a graphic organizer like the one at right with the information for their imaginary scenario.

Section 3: Foreign Policy and International Institutions

SUPPORTING ENGLISH-LANGUAGE INSTRUCTION

Analyzing Information (30 minutes)
Supporting a Main Idea Have students read the text under the heading "The United Nations." Discuss with students the role and the organization of the United Nations. Then have each student create a graphic organizer like the one at right on his or her own sheet of paper. Instruct students to label the boxes on the left with the different groups and organizations within the UN. Have students write a description of the responsibilities of each group in the boxes on the right.

Teacher Tip
Have students look at the examples of president as chief diplomat and president as commander in chief that are illustrated in the chart in their textbook. Discuss with students how each example reflects the president's power to shape foreign policy.

Teacher Tip
Direct students to the Web sites of presidential libraries as a starting point for their research.

Graphic Organizer

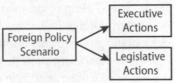

Graphic Organizer
The United Nations

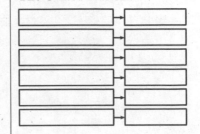

If time permits, you may have students add more boxes to the graphic organizer and identify other international institutions and their responsibilities.

Section 4: Foreign Policy Challenges

SUPPORTING SPECIAL EDUCATION INSTRUCTION

Connecting Information (30 minutes)
Assembling a Foreign Policy Time Line Have students read the text under the heading "Past Foreign Policy Challenges." Encourage students to take notes as they read. Then have students use the events they read about to make a time line titled "History of U.S. Foreign Policy." Instruct students to record the key events and shifts in U.S. foreign policy, along with the approximate date for each event. Ask for volunteers to share their time lines with the class.

SUPPORTING ENGLISH-LANGUAGE INSTRUCTION

Summarizing Information (30 minutes)
Analyzing Challenges to Modern Foreign Policy
Have students read the text under the heading "Transitions to Democracy." Help students understand that one key influence on modern foreign policy has been the establishment of democratic governments throughout the world, a process known as democratization. Instruct students to draw a graphic organizer like the one at right on their own sheet of paper. Then have students complete the graphic organizer by summarizing the information for each world region in two or three succinct sentences. Alternatively, students may create illustrations that summarize and help them remember the information.

Teacher Tip
You may want to have students work in small groups to identify the key events and when each event occurred. Then have students work independently to create their own time lines.

Graphic Organizer
Transitions to Democracy

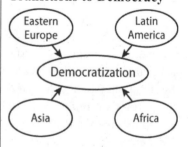

Section 1: Democratic Governments

SUPPORTING ADVANCED/GIFTED AND TALENTED INSTRUCTION
Expanding Information (45 minutes)
Examining an Emerging Democracy After students have read the text under the heading "Emerging Democracies," lead a class discussion about the difficulties some nations face as they transition from an authoritarian government to a more democratic government. Have each student select a country that is transitioning to democracy and ask students to use the library, Internet, and other sources to research the steps that country is taking to implement a democratic government. Have students write a one-page essay detailing the move toward democracy in their selected country. Ask volunteers to share their findings with the class.

SUPPORTING SPECIAL EDUCATION INSTRUCTION
Expanding Information (45 minutes)
Comparing Democratic Governments Have each student select a democratic country to research. Then have students use the library, Internet, or other sources to learn about the government of their assigned country. Instruct students to research the type of government, constitution, branches of government, heads of state, and political parties for their assigned country. Have students create a chart like the one at right to compile their findings. Then have students complete the same information for the United States. Ask volunteers to share their findings with the class, focusing on the ways in which the two countries are similar and different.

Resources
- Spanish Chapter Summaries Audio CD Program
- Differentiated Instruction Modified Worksheets and Tests on the Teacher One Stop™.
  - Vocabulary Flash Cards
  - Vocabulary Activities
  - Chapter Review
  - Section Quizzes
  - Chapter Test
- Advanced Placement Review and Activities

Graphic Organizer
Comparing Democratic Governments

Country		
Type of Government		
Constitution		
Branches		
Heads of State		
Political Parties		

Section 2: Authoritarian Governments

SUPPORTING ENGLISH-LANGUAGE INSTRUCTION

Interpreting Information (30 minutes)
Understanding Vocabulary Terms Write the following terms for students to see: *authoritarian*, *theocracy*, *dictatorship*, *totalitarianism*, *communism*, *propaganda*, and *fascism*. Organize students into small groups and assign each group a term from the list. Have students use dictionaries, their textbook, and other sources to help define their term. Then have each group explain its term to the class. Instruct students to use a chart like the one at right to take notes on each group's explanation.

Graphic Organizer
Vocabulary Terms

Term	Definition

SUPPORTING SPECIAL EDUCATION INSTRUCTION

Categorizing Information (45 minutes)
Understanding Characteristics of Authoritarian Systems Have students read the Quick Facts chart titled "Characteristics of Authoritarian Systems." Then have each student select one of the authoritarian governments discussed in this section. Instruct students to create a chart similar to the one at right. Have students complete the chart by finding examples of each of the characteristics listed. Have students use the library, Internet, or other sources to find appropriate examples of each characteristic. Encourage students to share their charts with the class.

Graphic Organizer
Authoritarian Systems

Characteristic	Examples
Few civil or human rights	
Limited citizen participation	
No freedom of expression	
Use of force	
Unlimited power of leaders	

Section 3: Economic Systems

SUPPORTING ENGLISH-LANGUAGE INSTRUCTION

Analyzing Information (20 minutes)
Examining Economic Systems Discuss with students the three economic systems covered in this section. Ask students to identify the characteristics of each system. Make a list of student responses for everyone to see. Then have students create a Venn diagram similar to the one at right. Instruct students to use the diagram to list the similarities and differences between capitalism and socialism. Ask volunteers to share their comparisons with the class.

Graphic Organizer
Comparing Economic Systems

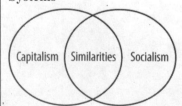

Lesson Plans for Differentiated Instruction

Section 1: States and the National Government

SUPPORTING ADVANCED/GIFTED AND TALENTED INSTRUCTION

Expanding Information (45 minutes)

Examining State Constitutions After students have read the text under the heading "State Constitutions," organize the class into several small groups. Assign each group a state listed in the chart "Constitutions and Amendments." Have each group use the library, Internet, or other sources to find the current constitution for its assigned state. Have students work together with their group to evaluate the state constitution. Remind students to examine the number of amendments, the types of laws covered in the constitution, and the length of the constitution. Then have each group conduct a five-minute presentation to the class in which group members describe the constitution of their assigned state and discuss its strengths and weaknesses.

SUPPORTING SPECIAL EDUCATION INSTRUCTION

Analyzing Information (30 minutes)

Examining Your State Constitution Organize the class into small groups and pass out copies of your state's constitution. Have each group skim through the constitution, making an outline of the constitution's major sections. Have students make note of when the constitution was written, how long it is, and how many amendments it has. Ask each group to rate the constitution in terms of how easy it is for the average citizen to read and understand. Then have each student write a letter to his or her state legislator, explaining the student's own thoughts on the constitution.

Section 2: State Government

SUPPORTING ENGLISH-LANGUAGE INSTRUCTION

Connecting Information (45 minutes)

Examining State Government Have students research their state government. Instruct students to use the library, Internet, or other sources to identify the structure of their state government. Then have students create graphic organizers like the one at right for each major branch of government. Encourage students to display their graphic organizers.

Resources

- Spanish Chapter Summaries Audio CD Program
- Differentiated Instruction Modified Worksheets and Tests on the Teacher One Stop™
  - Vocabulary Flash Cards
  - Vocabulary Activities
  - Chapter Review
  - Section Quizzes
  - Chapter Test
- Advanced Placement Review and Activities

Teacher Tip

Remind students of proper protocol for writing to public officials. Remind students to keep their letters short and to the point. You may wish to have students research the correct style for addressing their legislators.

Graphic Organizer

Organization of State Government

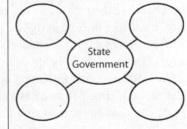

SUPPORTING ADVANCED/GIFTED AND TALENTED INSTRUCTION
Expanding Information (45 minutes)
Researching State Finances To help students learn more about state government, have them research their state's services and finances. Have students use the library, Internet, or other sources to identify the services provided by their state. Have students create a list of services by category. For each category, have students identify several specific services. For example, under the category of education, students might list purchasing textbooks. Then have students research the state budget to identify what percentage of the state budget goes to provide the services in each category.

Teacher Tip
Have students use their data to create pie charts illustrating the categories of services the state provides and the percentage of the state budget that goes to each service.

Section 3: Local Government and Citizen Participation

SUPPORTING ENGLISH-LANGUAGE INSTRUCTION
Interpreting Information (30 minutes)
Understanding Vocabulary Before students read the section, help them learn the key terms they will encounter in the section. Start by writing the key terms for students to see. Have students copy the terms in a chart like the one at right. Using the glossary in the back of their textbook for reference, students should write down the definition for each key term. When students have finished, go over each term, explaining the meaning of each term in language the students can understand. Finally, have students complete their charts by writing down the meaning of each term in their own words.

Graphic Organizer
Key Terms

Term	Definition	Meaning
Counties		

Graphic Organizer
Understanding Local Government

SUPPORTING SPECIAL EDUCATION INSTRUCTION
Expanding Information (45 minutes)
Researching Local Government Have students learn more about their local government by researching the structure of their town, city, or village government. Have students use their own sheet of paper to create a graphic organizer like the one at right. Then have students use the library, Internet, or other sources to research the type and organization of their local government, the names and offices of key officials, and important ordinances that are currently in the news. If time permits, have students contact a local official and ask questions about his or her job.

Foundations of Democracy

FOUNDATIONS OF DEMOCRACY

The Center for Civic Education's *Foundations of Democracy* is a student resource designed to help students examine the fundamental values of our government. Organized around the concepts of authority, privacy, responsibility, and justice, *Foundations of Democracy* challenges students to think for themselves, to develop reasoned positions, and to articulate and defend their views.

The *Foundations of Democracy* student consumable is designed to be integrated into courses in U.S. government, civics, history, and other social science courses. *Foundations of Democracy* will help prepare your students to be active and effective citizens in our constitutional democracy.

Foundations of Democracy may be taught in its entirety, or you may select specific concepts as they relate to general curriculum goals and learning outcomes. The concepts need not be taught in any particular order. Each of the four concepts in this curriculum is organized into multiple units of study, each designed to answer a fundamental question about the nature and application of that concept. Below are the guiding questions for the units of study within each concept area.

AUTHORITY

Unit One: What is Authority?

Unit Two: How Can We Evaluate Candidates for Positions of Authority?

Unit Three: How Can We Evaluate Rules and Laws?

Unit Four: What are the Benefits and Costs of Authority?

Unit Five: What should be the Scope and Limits of Authority?

PRIVACY

Unit One: What is the Importance of Privacy?

Unit Two: What should be the Scope and Limits of Privacy?

RESPONSIBILITY

Unit One: What is Responsibility?

Unit Two: What are the Benefits and Costs of Fulfilling Responsibility?

JUSTICE

Unit One: What is Justice?

Unit Two: What is Distributive Justice?

The Teaching Tips and Answer Key, which begins on the following page, includes answers to selected Critical Thinking Exercises and other questions from *Foundations of Democracy*. Also included are strategies for incorporating each lesson in your classroom instruction. The Teaching Tips and Answer Key section is organized by lesson.

Authority

Lesson 1
CRITICAL THINKING EXERCISE
Distinguishing between Authority and Power without Authority
What Do *You* Think?

1. Kneecappers: maimed criminals and other citizens; threatened citizens; Police: arrested suspected kneecappers; investigated kangaroo courts

2. Help students understand that the police had the authority to do what they did because the law or custom gave government officials that right. Make sure students understand that individuals who exercise authority over others have the right to do so according to custom, law, or principles of morality. You may want to make the point that, although an individual may have the right to exercise authority in a certain situation, that does not guarantee that he or she will exercise that authority justly, fairly, properly, or morally.

3. Help students understand that the members of the Irish Republican Army had no authority. They do not have a right to control or direct other people's behavior. Make sure students understand that while power is the ability to control or direct others, individuals who do so but lack the right (according to custom, law, or principles or morality) are said to be using power without authority.

CRITICAL THINKING EXERCISE
Describing the Difference between Authority and Power without Authority
What Do *You* Think?

Situations 1, 3, 4, 5, and 10 are examples of authority. Situations 2, 6, 7, 8, and 9 are examples of power without authority.

USING THE LESSON
The activities suggested in "Using the Lesson" on p. 6 of the text reinforce or extend what students have learned about distinguishing between authority and power without authority. You may have students work individually or in small groups to complete these activities. Have students share their work with the class.

Lesson 2
USING THE LESSON
The activities suggested in "Using the Lesson" on p. 11 of the text are designed to reinforce or extend what students learned about sources of authority and the importance of understanding the sources of authority in particular situations. You may have students work individually or in small groups to complete the activities suggested.

Lesson 3
CRITICAL THINKING EXERCISE
Evaluating and Taking a Position on the Necessity of Government
What Do *You* Think?
Below are some answers students might make to these questions:

1. According to John Locke, what problems can arise when there is no government authority?
   a. Life would be dangerous and full of fear
   b. The enjoyment of freedom would be uncertain because people would always be open to attack from others
   c. There would be no protection of personal property
   d. There would be no established system of law that all people have agreed upon and that all people know
   e. There would be no standard of right and wrong which could be used to settle arguments
   f. There would be no judge with authority to settle arguments
   g. There would be no person or group of people with the authority to enforce the law

2. What does Locke say is the source of government authority?

People seek others who share their need for security and join with them in an effort to protect their lives, their liberty, and their property. They join together under the protection and authority of government. They agree on the administration of punishment according to a system of rules. This is the source of legislative, judicial, and executive authority.

3. What was Thoreau's position about the need for governmental authority?

Students should recall Thoreau's position that, when people are ready for such a state of affairs, government will not be necessary. He viewed government as an ill-chosen expedient which was not really very helpful and was easily abused.

4. What changes in society would have to occur to make people ready to live without government?

Encourage students to speculate. They might suggest that for a society to function without government such things as the following would be required: a widespread sense of responsibility, of cooperation, and of fairness, agreed-upon rules of behavior, and procedures for managing conflict.

CRITICAL THINKING EXERCISE
Evaluating the Use of Authority
What Do *You* Think?

Some responses students might offer include the following:

1. How was authority used to deal with the water supply contamination problem?

a. the EPA enacted regulations designed to prevent problems involving pollution

b. the EPA negotiated with the company to reach a solution to the problem as it existed

c. the EPA filed suit against the company for failure to comply with the pollution control regulations that the EPA was responsible for enforcing

d. the courts heard the case and handed down a decision

2. What problems might have arisen if there had been no effective authority to deal with this situation?

a. the company could have continued operations and the water would have continued to be contaminated

b. the company could have tried to prevent contamination but the pollutants might not have been controlled effectively or soon enough to prevent the undesirable effects

c. the people in the area could have become ill

d. effective controls on the company's actions would have been difficult to impose and enforce

e. community members might have been tempted to use violence or other forms of coercion

3. In what other ways could authority have been used to deal with the problems in this situation?

a. the EPA could have enacted new regulations to control contamination without putting undue economic hardship on the company

b. the federal government could have assisted in research to find quicker and more effective ways of disposing of potential pollutants

USING THE LESSON

The activities suggested in "Using the Lesson" on p. 14 of the text reinforce or extend what students have learned about how we can use authority to resolve problems in society. You may have students work individually or in small groups to complete these activities. Have students share their work with the class.

Lesson 4
USING THE LESSON

The activities suggested in "Using the Lesson" on p. 18 of the text reinforce or extend what students have learned about selecting a person for a position of authority. When completing each of the activities, encourage students to use the intellectual tools for selecting persons for positions of authority. Have students share their work with the class.

Lesson 5
USING THE LESSON

The activities suggested in "Using the Lesson" on p. 25 of the text are designed to reinforce or extend what students learned about using intellectual tools for selecting a person for a position of authority. Encourage students to use the intellectual tools to complete these activities. You may have students work individually or in small groups.

Lesson 6
USING THE LESSON

The activities suggested in "Using the Lesson" on p. 28 of the text reinforce or extend what students learned about the characteristics of a good rule and using intellectual tools for evaluating rules. You may have students work on these activities individually or in small groups. Have students share their work with the class.

Lesson 7
USING THE LESSON

The activities suggested in "Using the Lesson" on p. 32 of the text reinforce or extend what students learned about the characteristics of a good rule and using intellectual tools for evaluating rules. You may have students work on these activities individually or in small groups. Have students share their work with the class.

Lesson 8
CRITICAL THINKING EXERCISE
Deciding Whether a Consequence Is a Benefit or Cost
What Do *You* Think?
Some responses students might offer during class discussion include the following:

Situation 1: An ordinance imposing a 10:30 p.m. curfew on people under the age of eighteen

a. people under the age of eighteen would have to be off the streets by 10:30 p.m. A cost.
b. since juveniles would be off the streets, juvenile crime might be diminished. A benefit.
c. if juvenile crime were diminished, people would feel safer. A benefit.
d. some places, such as movie theaters, would lose business because juveniles would not be able to be out after curfew. A cost.
e. the school would not be able to schedule events, such as dances or football games, which would extend past curfew. A cost.
f. there might be an increased financial cost involved in enforcing the curfew. A cost.

Situation 2: A law setting high standards for disposal of industrial wastes

a. there might be less pollution in the environment. A benefit.
b. if there were less pollution, natural resources might be better preserved. A benefit.
c. some people might be fined for not complying with the new pollution control standards. A cost.
d. it would cost some businesses a lot of money to convert their present systems over to comply with the new pollution control standards. A cost.
e. the freedom of some businesses to pursue their interests would be limited. A cost.

Situation 3: A law making it illegal to print and sell materials depicting acts of violence

a. people would not have the freedom to print, sell, or read such material. A cost.
b. the law might give too much power to those who are to enforce it, if the law does not state specifically what kinds of stories or pictures cannot be printed or sold. A cost.
c. there might be fewer criminal acts because inflammatory stories about violence would not be circulating. A benefit.
d. people who publish such literature would lose money. A cost.

USING THE LESSON

The activities suggested in "Using the Lesson" on p. 36 of the text reinforce or extend what students learned about identifying the consequences of the use of authority and classifying those consequences as benefits or costs. You may have students complete the activities individually or in small groups. Have students share their work with the class.

Lesson 9
CRITICAL THINKING EXERCISE
Evaluating the Benefits and Costs of Authority
What Do *You* Think?

The following are some possible responses students might offer:

What might be the consequences of the trial judge's exercise of authority in this case?

a. the defendant was not allowed to be present during part of his trial. A cost.

b. the defendant was not allowed to act as his own attorney even though he wished to do so. A cost.

c. the fact that the defendant was shackled during part of the trial might have influenced the jurors against him. A cost.

d. the trial was conducted in an orderly and peaceful fashion. A benefit.

e. the judge's actions might serve as an example to others who might attempt to disrupt judicial proceedings. A benefit.

f. since the judge's action was upheld, the authority of the court was strengthened. This would enable other judges to deal with disruption in their courts in a similar manner. A benefit.

USING THE LESSON

The activities suggested in "Using the Lesson" on p. 39 of the text reinforce or extend what students learned about identifying the consequences of the use of authority and classifying those consequences as benefits or costs. You may have students complete the activities individually or in small groups. Have students share their work with the class.

Lesson 10
CRITICAL THINKING EXERCISE
Evaluating Errors in Designing a Position of Authority
What Do *You* Think?

1. The following are responses students might offer:

a. Governor of Confusion: The position of governor has too many responsibilities for one person to do well.

b. Legislator of the State of Perpetua: Since there is no way to remove legislators from office, there is no way for people to hold them accountable for what they do.

c. Hall Monitor: Hall monitors have been given too much power.

d. Major of Agoraphobia City: The mayor made it impossible for the public to present their ideas to him.

e. Traffic Control Officers: The officers do not have resources needed to do their job.

f. The Grand Inquisitor: There is no provision for fair and humane procedures in the exercise of the position's authority.

2. Some responses students might offer include the following:

A well-developed position of authority should

a. not be overburdened with duties

b. be designed with sufficient accountability

c. be assigned appropriate power(s)

d. be designed to allow public input

e. provide enough resources to do the job

f. require fair and humane procedures in the exercise of its authority

g. be subject to periodic review

h. have clear limits on the power allocated to it

i. be designed so that it will not interfere unnecessarily with important values, such as individual dignity, freedom of speech, privacy, etc.

j. be adaptable to changing circumstances

USING THE LESSON

The activities suggested in "Using the Lesson" on p. 42 of the text reinforce or extend what students have learned about evaluating positions of authority. Encourage students to use the criteria they learned during the lesson in completing these exercises. You may have students work individually or in small groups to complete these activities. Have students share their work with the class.

Lesson 11
USING THE LESSON

The activities suggested in "Using the Lesson" on p. 45 of the text reinforce or extend what students have learned about evaluating positions of authority. Encourage students to use the criteria they learned during the lesson in completing these exercises. You may have students work individually or in small groups to complete these activities. Have students share their work with the class.

CRITICAL THINKING EXERCISE
Evaluating a Position of Authority
Intellectual Tool Chart for Evaluating Positions of Authority
Some responses students might offer include the following:

1. Ship's captain in the mid-19th century
2. To be in charge of the ship and the crew during the voyage
3. Students should speculate about whether it is necessary to have a captain and what might happen if there were no captain. They might also discuss other ways to achieve the purpose stated above.
4. See job description on p. 44 of the text.
5. By enforcing stricter discipline the captain might have been ensuring the safety of the ship and its cargo and the completion of a safe, successful voyage; He would maintain order and safety of the crew; Some sailors were punished without opportunity for a fair hearing on the charges; Some sailors were subjected to excessive and cruel punishment
6. Responsible for the safety of the cargo, the ship, and the vessel; Resources are sufficient to carry out his duties; Excessive power, i.e., there are no clear limits on the captain's power; Insufficient accountability; i.e., there do not appear to

be any effective ways on the ship to review the captain's conduct and to correct wrongful acts on his part; Unfairness of procedures employed, i.e., there appear to be no limits to ensure that the captain's power to punish is used fairly, such as requirement of due process or restrictions against cruel and unusual punishment; Inaccessibility, i.e., there do not appear to be any procedures by which the sailors can make their opinions known and have them considered in setting policy for the ship; Unnecessary interference with important values, i.e., the captain's actions interfere unnecessarily with the sailors' right to speak or act freely which undermines their sense of dignity

7. Students may present and explain a number of options. They should be encouraged to explain the benefits and costs of the alternatives they select. Changes they might suggest include: Putting designated limits on the power of the captain, including requirements for fair procedures, prohibitions on cruel punishments, and protections for sailors' rights; Instituting systematic procedures whereby the captain's conduct would be reviewed and action taken to correct misuse of power; Instituting procedures whereby sailors have ways to make their opinions known to the captain and those who are reviewing the captain's conduct

8. Students should write their final conclusions and one or two sentences justifying their positions.

Lesson 12
USING THE LESSON

The activities suggested in "Using the Lesson" on p. 50 of the text reinforce or extend what students have learned about evaluating positions of authority. Encourage students to use the criteria they learned during the lesson in completing these exercises. You may have students work individually or in small groups. Have students share their work with the class.

Lesson 13

USING THE LESSON

The activities suggested in "Using the Lesson" on p. 52 of the text reinforce or extend what students have learned about creating positions of authority. Encourage students to use the intellectual tools they learned during the lesson in completing these exercises. You may have students work individually or in small groups to complete these activities. Have students share their work with the class.

Lesson 14

CONCLUDING THE AUTHORITY CURRICULUM

This concludes the study of the Authority curriculum. It will be valuable to both you and your students to reflect upon and evaluate the total experience with this concept in *Foundations of Democracy*, including the content and instruction methods. Remind students that they should not only reflect upon and evaluate their own experiences, but also those of the class. Have students share their responses with the class.

Privacy

Lesson 1

USING THE LESSON

The activities suggested in "Using the Lesson" on p. 65 of the text are designed to reinforce or extend what students have learned about identifying common objects of privacy and the reasons why people may wish to have privacy in specific situations. When working on any of the activities suggested, encourage students to refer to the five questions used in the critical thinking exercise: 1. **Why** is the situation an example of privacy; 2. **Who** wants to keep something private; 3. What is the **object of privacy**; 4. From **whom** is something being kept private; and, 5. **Why** do you suppose the person wanted privacy? You may want to have students work on these activities individually or in small groups. Have students share their work with the class.

Collecting news clippings, as suggested in activity 2, can be used to initiate a bulletin board project for the class. Students can be encouraged to contribute newspaper and magazine articles during the next few weeks of instruction.

Lesson 2

USING THE LESSON

The activities suggested in "Using the Lesson" on p. 67 of the text are designed to reinforce or extend what students have learned about people's privacy behavior. When working on any of the activities suggested, encourage students to use the terms **isolation, secrecy, confidentiality,** and **exclusion.** You may have students work on these activities individually or in small groups. Have students share their work with the class.

Lesson 3

USING THE LESSON

The activities suggested in "Using the Lesson" on p. 71 of the text are designed to reinforce or extend what students have learned about institutional privacy or secrecy. When working on any of the activities suggested, encourage students to analyze: 1. what objects organizations and institutions might want to keep private or secret; 2. from whom they want to keep them private or secret; 3. how they keep the objects private or secret; and 4. why they might want to keep the objects private or secret. You may have students work on these activities individually or in small groups. Have students share their work with the class.

Lesson 4

CRITICAL THINKING EXERCISE
Describing Relevant Considerations
What Do *You* Think?
Some possible responses might include the following:
  1. **No.** Officer McFadden acted after observing the two men from across the street.

2. **Yes.** Because of their suspicious behavior, Officer McFadden had a right to stop the men and to frisk them for weapons they might use to attack him.

3. Both Mr. Terry and Mr. Chilton claimed that the search violated their Fourth Amendment rights.

4. Officer McFadden initiated the stop and frisk action after observing the behavior of the two men. Their repeated pattern of behavior created a reasonable suspicion and obligated the officer to stop and frisk the two men. The search consisted solely of patting of the outer clothing for concealed objects that might be used in an assault. Only after discovering the object did Officer McFadden place his hands in the pockets of the men he searched.

USING THE LESSON

The activities suggested in "Using the Lesson" on p. 76 of the text are designed to help students reinforce or extend what they have learned about using intellectual tools to develop a position on an issue of privacy. The activities may be assigned individually or in small groups.

Lesson 5
USING THE LESSON

The activities suggested in "Using the Lesson" on p. 78 of the student text are designed to help students reinforce or extend what they have learned about using intellectual tools to evaluate different positions and to take and defend a position on an issue of privacy. During each activity, encourage students to use the five-step procedure for evaluating different positions and for taking and defending a position on an issue of privacy. Students may complete these exercises by working individually or in small groups. Have students share their work with the class.

Lesson 6
USING THE LESSON

The activities suggested in "Using the Lesson" on p. 83 of the student text are designed to

help students reinforce or extend what they have learned about using intellectual tools to evaluate different positions and to take and defend a position on an issue of privacy. The activities may be assigned individually. Encourage students to use the five-step procedure for evaluating different positions and for taking and defending a position on an issue of privacy.

Lesson 7
USING THE LESSON

The activities suggested in "Using the Lesson" on p. 87 of the student text are designed to help students reinforce or extend what they have learned about using intellectual tools to evaluate different positions and to take and defend their own position on an issue of privacy. The activities may be assigned individually. Encourage students to use the five-step procedure for evaluating different positions and for taking and defending a position on an issue of privacy.

Lesson 8
USING THE LESSON

The activities suggested in "Using the Lesson" on p. 90 of the student text are designed to help students reinforce or extend what they have learned about establishing a policy to deal with issues that might arise repeatedly. The activities may be assigned individually.

Responsibility
Lesson 1
USING THE LESSON

The activities suggested in "Using the Lesson" on p. 96 of the text are designed to reinforce or extend what students have learned about identifying sources of responsibility and how people assume responsibilities. You may have students complete these exercises by working individually or in small groups. Ask students to share their work with the class.

Lesson 2
USING THE LESSON
The activities suggested in "Using the Lesson" on p. 101 of the text are designed to reinforce or extend what students have learned about identifying sources of responsibility, how people assume responsibilities, and rewards and penalties for fulfilling or not fulfilling responsibilities. Encourage students to use the "Responsibility Study Chart" when working on these activities. You may have students complete these exercises by working individually or in small groups. Ask students to share their work with the class.

Lesson 3
USING THE LESSON
The activities suggested in "Using the Lesson" on p. 105 of the text are designed to reinforce or extend what students have learned about benefits and costs of fulfilling responsibility. You may have students complete these exercises by working individually or in small groups. Ask students to share their work with the class.

Lesson 4
CRITICAL THINKING EXERCISE
Evaluating, Taking, and Defending a Position on the Use of Solar Energy

1. Students should recognize that the city is considering taking on all the responsibilities inherent in developing and maintaining a solar energy project.
2. Students should identify and infer the consequences of taking on these responsibilities, including:
a. an expenditure for the city of a large sum of money
b. local taxes would most likely have to be increased to pay for the project
c. the federal government would pay for half the cost of the project
d. because of the local climate, the old systems of heating and air conditioning would still have to be maintained

e. the use of solar energy, instead of coal, gas, or nuclear reactors, is safe and causes less pollution of the environment
f. the project will create new jobs in the community
g. the system would be cheaper to run and eventually provide a small savings to taxpayers

3-4. Students should classify each of the consequences as benefits or costs and explain the reasons for their classifications.
5. Help students understand the idea of relative importance and the reasons why people may have different views about the relative importance of the benefits and costs of fulfilling responsibilities in specific situations.

USING THE LESSON
The activities suggested in "Using the Lesson" on p. 109 of the text are designed to reinforce or extend what students have learned about benefits and costs of fulfilling responsibility. You may have students complete these exercises by working individually or in small groups. Ask students to share their work with the class.

Justice
Lesson 1
CRITICAL THINKING EXERCISE
Identifying Issues of Distributive, Corrective, and Procedural Justice
What Do *You* Think?

The following are possible responses students might offer:
1. distributive justice: situations 2, 5, 6, 12; corrective justice: situations 1, 8, 11; procedural justice: situations 3, 4, 7, 9, 10
2. Encourage students to explain what they think is fair or unfair about each of the situations. Encourage examination and evaluation of the various positions that different people might take about fairness in each situation.

3. Discussion of this question should help reinforce the reasons why we divide issues of justice into three categories and the concept of intellectual tools. For background information useful in guiding students' discussion of these questions and evaluating responses, you may want to preview the intellectual tools in Unit Two.

4. This question is designed to focus students' attention on the relevance of the subject and of the three categories of justice to their daily lives. Encourage students to relate at least one situation they have experienced or observed to the issues raised by each of the situations described in the exercise.

USING THE LESSON

The activities suggested in "Using the Lesson" on p. 115 of the text are designed to reinforce or extend what students have learned about categorizing issues of justice such as **distributive, corrective,** or **procedural justice.** When working on any of the activities suggested, encourage students to

1. identify the category of justice involved

2. think about what might be fair or unfair about the situation

3. identify similar situations they might have experienced or observed

You can have students work on the three activities suggested in "Using the Lesson" individually or in small groups. Have the students share their work with the class.

Lesson 2
CRITICAL THINKING EXERCISE
Examining Justice—A National Idea
What Do *You* Think?

1. **Group 1**: distributive—Declaration of Independence, Amendment I; corrective—Amendment VIII

    Group 2: distributive—Amendment XIV; Article I, Section 9, Clause 3; procedural—Amendment VII, Amendment XIV

    Group 3: distributive—Amendment XXVI; corrective—Article II, Section 2;

procedural—Article I, Section 9, Clause 2; Amendment V

Group 4: distributive—Article III, Section 3, Clause 2; Amendment XIII, Section 1; Amendment XXIV, Section 1; corrective—Article III, Section 3, Clause 2; procedural—Amendment VI

Group 5: distributive—Amendment IV; Amendment XIX, Section 1; procedural: Article III, Section 2, Clause 3; Article IV, Section 2; Amendment IV

distributive justice: benefits and burdens—Generally, the excerpts classified as distributive justice include the distribution of benefits such as individual rights (life, liberty, happiness; freedom of religious belief, speech, press, assembly; privacy) and political equality (voting rights, equal protection of the laws); values or interests—Generally, these excerpts protect and promote human dignity, equal opportunity, individual freedom of thought and deed, interest in the free exchange of ideas, popular control of government, and protection of diversity and individuality.

corrective justice: responses—Generally, the excerpts classified as corrective justice include such responses as freedom from cruel and unusual punishments, pardons and reprieves, and punishment for treason; values and interests—Generally, these excerpts protect and promote human dignity.

procedural justice: procedures—Generally, the excerpts classified as procedural justice include such procedures as due process of law (grand jury indictment, informed of the nature and cause of the accusation, speedy trial, right to counsel, confronted by witnesses, protection from double jeopardy, etc.) and procedures for gathering information and making decisions (impartial jury, public trial, unreasonable searches and seizures, protection from self-incrimination, no deprivation of life, liberty, property without due process of law, etc.); values or interests—Generally, these excerpts protect and promote the fair and open function of government, human dignity, individual liberty, privacy, and property.

2. Article III, Section 3, Clause 2; Amendment IV; Amendment XIV. Reasonable positions may be taken that other excerpts serve more than one category of issues of justice. These should be discussed.

USING THE LESSON

The activities suggested in "Using the Lesson" on p. 119 of the text are designed to reinforce or extend what students have learned about categorizing issues of justice such as **distributive, corrective,** or **procedural.** When working on any of the activities suggested, encourage students to

1. identify the category of justice involved
2. think about what might be fair or unfair about the situation
3. identify what fundamental principles, values, and interests might be involved

You can have students work on the activities suggested in "Using the Lesson" individually or in small groups. Have the students share their work with the class.

Lesson 3
USING THE LESSON

The activities suggested in "Using the Lesson" on p. 124 of the text are designed to reinforce or extend what students have learned about the intellectual tools for distributive justice. The activities give students practice in applying the principle of similarity and the considerations of need, capacity, and desert to specific situations. When working on any of the activities suggested, encourage students to do the following:

1. apply the principle of similarity
2. apply the considerations of need, capacity, and desert
3. consider other values and interests in developing a position on an issue of distributive justice.

You may have students work on these activities individually or in small groups.

Lesson 4
USING THE LESSON

The activities suggested in "Using the Lesson" on p. 129 of the text are designed to reinforce or extend what students have learned about using the intellectual tools for distributive justice. You may have students work on these activities individually or in small groups. Have the students share their work with the class.

Lesson 5
USING THE LESSON

The activities suggested in "Using the Lesson" on p. 133 of the text are designed to reinforce or extend what students have learned about using the intellectual tools for distributive justice. You may have students work on these activities individually or in small groups.

Interactive Reader
and Study Guide

INTERACTIVE READER AND STUDY GUIDE

The *Interactive Reader and Study Guide* is an excellent tool for helping students who need additional support in order to grasp the concepts presented in *Holt McDougal United States Government: Principles in Practice*. Used in conjunction with the textbook, the *Interactive Reader and Study Guide* can help students master the content they need to know.

The graphic summary of each chapter is particularly valuable for students who are better able to master information if they are presented with a visual representation of it. Comprehension and Critical Thinking Questions measure how much of the chapter students recall and can be a guide to determine which of the chapter's sections may need more attention than others.

For each section, the *Interactive Reader and Study Guide* provides the Main Idea, Key Terms, a Section Summary graphic organizer, and a detailed Section Summary. In the margin of each page are questions and activities designed to help students interact with the text in order to better recall the information they have read.

The *Interactive Reader and Study Guide* can help you ensure that all of your students master the information covered in *Holt McDougal United States Government: Principles in Practice*. You can also use the questions to review material with the class as a whole, or as a starting point for class discussions on issues raised in the chapter.

Answers to each of the questions in the *Interactive Reader and Study Guide* are provided in the Answer Key that follows.

Teacher Management System

Chapter 1: Foundations of Government

CHAPTER SUMMARY

1. liberty, equality, and self-government
2. because of the different theories on which government is based and how power is organized.
3. Answers will vary. Possible answer: to protect people's liberty, equality, and self-government

SECTION 1
Taking Notes

Possible responses for purposes of government: ensure national security, maintain order, resolve conflict, provide services, and provide for the public good.

Section Summary

1. Answers will vary. Possible answers: passing legislation to fund education; improving relations with a foreign country.
2. Government is also expected to enforce laws and punish those who do not follow them.
3. Answers will vary. Possible answers: building roads, providing public housing.
4. People collectively agreed to submit to the authority of the state.

SECTION 2
Taking Notes

In the 'Form" column, students should list the forms of government described in the summary, such as monarchy, dictatorship, oligarchy, direct democracy, republic, unitary system, federal system, confederal system, presidential system, and parliamentary system. In the "Details" column, students should provide definitions of or information about each form of government.

Section Summary

1. The monarch is more powerful in an absolute monarchy.
2. In a direct democracy, the people make political decisions themselves. In a republic, the people elect representatives to make these decisions for them.
3. In a federal system, regional governments share power with the national government. In a confederal system, the regional governments are much more powerful than the national government.
4. Since the legislature and the prime minister are part of the same, single branch of government and are not subject to separation of powers, they do not always need the agreement of the other to get things done.

SECTION 3
Taking Notes

Possible responses for democracy in the U.S.: ideals of American democracy (liberty, equality, self-government); principles of American democracy (rule of law, worth of the individual, majority rule, minority rights, compromise, citizen participation); free enterprise system

Section Summary

1. Freedom of speech allows people to say what they want, as long as it does not hurt others.
2. Answers will vary, but should discuss the equal treatment of all people under the law.
3. By protecting the liberties and equality of those not in the majority, liberal democracy protects two of the three ideals central to American democracy.
4. Answers will vary. Possible response: because competition can develop more easily if the government does not too closely regulate producers

Chapter 2: Origins of American Government

CHAPTER SUMMARY

1. new British policies
2. Possible answer: No, I was not surprised, since it makes sense that a document that controls the structure of the government would be controversial.
3. Answers will vary, but students should discuss how the compromises were necessary to ensure a government with none of the weaknesses that the government under the Articles experienced.

SECTION 1
Taking Notes

Answers will vary, but students should discuss ideas that were part of the colonists' heritage and knowledge, such as representative government and republicanism, in the left column, and events involving these ideas, such as the passage of the Fundamental Orders of Connecticut, in the right column.

Section Summary

1. representative government, individual rights, limited government
2. Possible answer: Royal colonies had less independence. Not all members of the legislature were elected by the colonists, as in a charter colony, and the colony was directly controlled by the king through a governor, unlike in a charter colony, where colonists had a say in the charter.
3. ideas about natural rights and economic and civil liberties

SECTION 2
Taking Notes

Answers will vary, but students should list at least three causes of the American Revolution, such as the Intolerable Acts, in the left box, and three effects of the war, such as the colonists gained their independence from Great Britain, in the right box.

Section Summary

1. to help member colonies defend themselves against Native Americans and nearby Dutch colonies
2. Possible answer: Since they did not have representation in Parliament, they did not feel that Parliament had the right to tax them.
3. war and independence
4. legislatures of elected representatives, as well as judicial and executive branches, and legislative and executive branches with limited powers; many also included bills of rights

SECTION 3
Taking Notes

Answers will vary, but students should list advantages of the Articles, allowed Congress to organize the western lands, in the left column and disadvantages of the Articles, such as national government could not raise money or help defend the country, in the right column.

Section Summary

1. when at least nine states had approved it
2. No. It did not have power to raise money, and the states did not contribute much.
3. Shays's Rebellion

SECTION 4
Taking Notes

Answers will vary, but students should discuss in the different circles the various plans and compromises reached during the Constitutional Convention, such as the Virginia and New Jersey Plans, the Great Compromise, and the Three-Fifths Compromise.

Section Summary

1. No. Each state received one vote.
2. how the population of a state would affect it membership in the national legislature
3. Three-fifths of the enslaved people in a state would be counted when determining a state's population.
4. They thought that the Constitution should include a bill of rights.

SECTION 5

Taking Notes

Answers will vary, but students should discuss in the different circles the groups and decisions that affected ratification, such as the Federalists, the Antifederalists, and the decision to include a bill of rights.

Section Summary

1. They claimed that the national government proposed by the Constitution would become too strong. They also criticized the absence of a bill of rights.
2. to defend the Constitution
3. as a series of amendments proposed by Congress and ratified by the states

Chapter 3: The Constitution

CHAPTER SUMMARY

1. form a more perfect union, establish justice, keep national peace, provide for the country's defense, promote the general welfare, and secure liberties
2. It helps the Constitution to change to meet the needs of the American people.
3. Answers will vary. Possible answer: Popular sovereignty is most important because it gives people a voice in their own government.

SECTION 1

Taking Notes

Students should fill in the six circles with the following phrases: popular sovereignty, limited government, separation of powers, checks and balances, judicial review, and federalism.

Section Summary

1. They were worried that citizens' rights would be suppressed.
2. By voting for who should represent them, people are choosing who should make up the government.
3. The Framers felt that government officials would not misuse their power if they had to follow the same laws as everyone else.

4. The judicial branch can declare legislation unconstitutional. The legislative branch can override vetoes.
5. The Tenth Amendment was necessary to fairly define which powers belonged to the national government and which powers belonged to the state governments.

SECTION 2

Taking Notes

Answer will vary. Possible answers in "Similarities" column: proposing amendment always requires supermajority; ratifying amendment always requires supermajority and action by state legislatures. Possible answers in "Differences" column: proposing amendment can take place only in Congress or at convention involving delegates not in Congress; ratifying amendment can take places inside or outside state legislatures.

Section Summary

1. Answers will vary. Possible answers: Jefferson: forward-thinking; Madison: cautious.
2. An amendment can be proposed by at least two-thirds of each house of Congress or by a national convention called by at least two-thirds of state legislatures; it can be ratified by three-fourths of state legislatures or a convention of at least three-fourths of the states.
3. Once ratified, an amendment becomes an official, permanent part of the Constitution. Therefore, it needs to be amended just like any other part of the Constitution.
4. Answers will vary. Possible answer: amendment that changes voting laws shows how certain groups of Americans have demanded and received fair treatment under the law.

SECTION 3

Taking Notes

Answers will vary. Possible answers: Congress and the president interpret and therefore expand reach of Constitution; Federal courts use judicial review to apply

Constitution to modern-day developments;
Political parties and various customs have
gradually affected the government structure
that the Constitution describes.

Section Summary
1. Congress has interpreted the Constitution
   to expand the lower level of the judicial
   branch; the Supreme Court has interpreted
   the Constitution in order to make powerful
   decisions on the constitutionality of laws.
2. Answers will vary. Possible answer: When
   the constitutionality of a law is being
   debated, people on either side of the debate
   may interpret parts of the Constitution
   differently.
3. Answers will vary. Possible answer:
   A political party helps a candidate get
   elected; if he or she wins, the candidate is
   then probably expected to help put the
   party's political agenda into place.
4. People believe that states with large
   populations should be assigned more
   senators than states with smaller
   populations.

Chapter 4: Federalism

CHAPTER SUMMARY
1. through fiscal federalism
2. Possible answer: a national crisis, such as
   a civil war
3. Possible answer: They may have felt that
   national government had become too
   powerful and that control over certain
   issues would be better retained by the
   states, which might be more familiar with
   how those issues affected different
   Americans.

SECTION 1
Taking Notes
Answers will vary, but students should list the
various powers of the national government in
the left circle, a description of the powers of
the state governments in the right circle, and
an explanation of concurrent and shared
powers in the overlapping section.

Section Summary
1. They gave the states all of the powers not
   granted to the national government.
2. only expressed powers are specifically
   listed in the Constitution
3. Possible answers: national—tax exports
   between states, spend money unless
   authorized by Congress, exercise powers
   reserved to the states, interfere with basic
   liberties; states—coin money, enter into
   treaties
4. discrimination by a state against a person
   from another state

SECTION 2
Taking Notes
Answers will vary, but students should explain
the influence of dual federalism, John
Marshall, cooperative federalism, creative
federalism, and new federalism.

Section Summary
1. the Supreme Court
2. because it was a necessary and proper
   action to take in order to carry out the
   expressed powers of regulating commerce
   and currency
3. Answers will vary but students should
   discuss how the federal government used
   grants—and the threat of a lack of
   grants—to get states to meet federal goals.
4. to return authority to the state
   governments

SECTION 3
Taking Notes
Answers will vary, but students should take
note of trends that characterize federalism
today, such as fiscal federalism, the use of
grants and mandates, as well as contemporary
issues (immigration, environment, health care,
and terrorism) that influence the relationship
between the national and state governments.

Section Summary
1. spending, taxing, and providing aid
2. Block grants are given for general
   purposes, so states can spend the money as
   they see fit; in contrast, federal mandates

require states to spend the money in a certain way to accomplish a specific goal.
3. States are more familiar with the problems facing their regional environments than the national government is.

Chapter 5: Congress: The Legislative Branch

CHAPTER SUMMARY
1. the Constitution
2. House representation is proportional to a states population, while Senate representation is equal.
3. Answers will vary, but students should provide support for their opinions.

SECTION 1
Taking Notes
Answers will vary, but students should note the groups that members of Congress represent in the first column, the bicameral design and apportionment process of Congress in the second column, and the various ways Congress checks the executive and judicial branches in the third column.

Section Summary
1. constituents, interest groups, country as a whole
2. to make sure that each House member represents approximately the same number of people
3. the Senate
4. Possible answer: It enables Congress to punish government officials who have abused their power.

SECTION 2
Taking Notes
Answers will vary, but students should list the expressed powers of Congress in one circle, the implied powers in the second circle, the nonlegislative powers in the third circle, and the powers denied to Congress in the fourth circle.

Section Summary
1. They are not specifically listed in the Constitution, as are the expressed powers.
2. direct taxes
3. testify
4. Possible answers: suspend the writ of habeas corpus, pass bills of attainder, pass ex post facto laws

SECTION 3
Taking Notes
Answers will vary, but students should note membership requirements and specific powers, an explanation of how reapportionment and gerrymandering affects the House, the different House leaders, and an explanation of the role and importance of House committees.

Section Summary
1. must be at least 25 years old, have been a U.S. citizen for at least seven years, and live in the state he or she represents
2. every 10 years, based on census results
3. Answers will vary, but students should discuss how the whip tries to sway members to vote as the party leadership wants them to vote.
4. Standing committees are permanent and select committees are usually temporary.

SECTION 4
Taking Notes
Answers will vary, but students should note membership requirements in the first circle, Senate leadership roles in the second circle, Senate committees in the third circle, and Senate rules and traditions in the fourth circle.

Section Summary
1. Elections take place every two years, when one-third of all seats are contested. The elections are open to all registered voters.
2. Senate majority leader
3. Under seniority rule, the senator who has served the longest on a committee becomes that committee's chair.
4. to prevent a vote in the Senate

SECTION 5
Taking Notes
Answers will vary, but students should note the various steps a bill goes through in the various boxes, such as referral, hearings in subcommittee, subcommittee report and recommendation, committee recommendation, and the different ways a bill is then debated, amended, and voted upon in each the House and the Senate.

Section Summary
1. to pass legislation that is unlikely to pass on its own
2. by listening to witnesses make statements on the bill
3. to reduce the quorum needed to conduct business
4. to reconcile different versions of the same bill in the House and the Senate

Chapter 6: The Presidency

CHAPTER SUMMARY
1. executive, diplomatic, military, judicial, and legislative powers
2. Possible response: Yes, it makes sense that a president would have to perform duties not specifically mentioned in the Constitution in order to carry out his or her official roles.
3. Answers will vary, but students should discuss how a more powerful president might need to increase the power of those who advise and work for him or her in order to successfully perform as president.

SECTION 1
Taking Notes
Possible responses for the "Formal" column: chief executive, chief administrator, commander in chief, foreign policy leader, chief agenda setter, at least 35 years of age, lived in the country for 14 years, natural-born citizen. Possible responses for the "Informal" column: chief of state, party leader, chief citizen, experience, impressive personal qualities.

Section Summary
1. chief executive, chief administrator, commander in chief, foreign policy leader, chief agenda setter
2. No, because she was born a French citizen, not a U.S. citizen.
3. Until the legislation was passed, there was no formal line of succession to follow if the president was unable to serve.
4. male, white, well-educated, Christian, usually military experience

SECTION 2
Taking Notes
Possible responses for the powers of the presidency: Executive Powers—appoint and remove, issue executive orders, use executive privilege; Diplomatic and Military Powers—negotiate treaties, make executive agreements, grant diplomatic recognition, call out armed forces; Legislative and Judicial Powers—propose legislation, veto legislation, nominate federal judges and justices, commute sentences, and grant reprieves, pardons, and amnesty.

Section Summary
1. Executive agreements do not require Senate consent.
2. the power to veto legislation
3. grant pardons, grant reprieves, grant amnesty, and commute sentences
4. The president can use the media to gather and maintain support.

SECTION 3
Taking Notes
Possible responses for the president's administration should note the Executive Office of the President, the chief of staff, the vice president, and the cabinet.

Section Summary
1. to coordinate issues of national security.
2. to organize the president's many advisers and assistants and executive programs and agencies
3. Recently, the vice president has become more of an adviser to the president and

now sometimes manages executive projects.

4. an interpretation of part of the Constitution

Chapter 7: The Executive Branch at Work

CHAPTER SUMMARY

1. administer areas of government responsibility
2. levying taxes and borrowing funds
3. Smaller agencies are needed to complete tasks that are too specific for executive agencies.

SECTION 1
Taking Notes

Possible responses for the federal bureaucracy should note the office of the vice president and the Executive Office of the President, as well as executive departments; independent executive agencies, independent regulatory commissions, and government corporations.

Section Summary

1. a clear, formal structure; a division of labor; and a set of rules and procedures by which it operates
2. The president gives out executive jobs to people he or she wants to reward, instead of people who were qualified for the jobs.
3. It made it illegal to hire people for civil-service jobs based on their party affiliation.

SECTION 2
Taking Notes

Possible response for "Independent Agencies": These agencies have legislative and judicial powers and sometimes can enforce own laws; Possible response for executive departments: These agencies are headed by cabinet members and contain internal, specific agencies. Possible response for the shared area: Both are created by Congress.

Section Summary

1. Congress confirms high-level position nominees and controls departments' duties, powers, and budgets.
2. Possible answers: Food and Drug Administration, Coast Guard, Secret Service
3. when it realizes that a private corporation would not be able to meet national need and still make a profit
4. passed legislation to check agencies

SECTION 3
Taking Notes

Possible responses for financing government: taxes, fees, nontax sources, borrowing

Section Summary

1. Since a proportional tax is applied the same against all income, it affects lower-income earners more than upper-income earners.
2. by selling bonds
3. the House and Senate Appropriations Committees
4. Spending money strategically and cutting taxes are both ways to stimulate the economy.

Chapter 8: The Federal Courts and the Judicial Branch

CHAPTER SUMMARY

1. The federal court system has a three-tier structure, with district courts on the bottom, courts of appeals in the middle, and the Supreme Court on top.
2. Since courts of appeals review cases first heard in district courts, it makes sense that they would be on a higher-level.
3. Answers will vary, but students should discuss how the Court will continue to issue landmark decisions that may affect everyday life and government.

SECTION 1
Taking Notes
Possible responses for federal courts: district courts, courts of appeal, and Supreme Court. Students should note details for each court.

Section Summary
1. They identify if a law has been broken and if penalties apply, they decide how to provide relief to those who have been harmed, and, if relevant, they determine the meaning of a specific law or part of the Constitution.
2. District courts make up the lowest tier and hear most federal criminal and civil cases. Courts of appeal make up the middle tier and hear appeals from district courts and some federal agencies. The Supreme Court makes up the highest tier and mainly hears appeals from the lower courts.
3. the judicial restraint end of the spectrum
4. the appointment process of judges, the amendment process, and the power to impeach and remove judges

SECTION 2
Taking Notes
Possible response for "District Courts" column: 94 courts, hear specific cases cited in Constitution and many criminal and civil cases. Possible response for "Courts of Appeal" column: 13 courts, hear cases on appeal from lower courts and some federal agencies, most rulings final. Possible response for "Other Courts" column: created by Congress, have very limited jurisdiction.

Section Summary
1. to determine whether the evidence presented to it is enough to file criminal charges
2. Congress created each special court.
3. The U.S. attorney represents the United States in federal cases in which the country or its people are affected.
4. Congress created each special court.

SECTION 3
Taking Notes
Possible response for "History" column: developed equal power to other two branches, *Dred Scott* decision checked Congress's power. Possible response for "Appointments" column: nominated by president and confirmed by Senate, most nominees have law background. Possible response for "Procedures" column: writ of certiorari orders review of a lower court's decision, justices can issue majority, concurrent, and dissenting opinions.

Section Summary
1. Possible answer: The decision showed that the Supreme Court had the power to check Congress.
2. Most have a background in law and share the same political party and judicial beliefs as the nominating president.
3. information about the nominee's personal and professional background, feelings on major political issues
4. No. Only five of the nine justices need to agree in order to issue a ruling.

Chapter 9: The Political Process

CHAPTER SUMMARY
1. Interest groups work to influence public opinion and lawmakers.
2. Answers will vary, but students should discuss a current issue and examine how public opinion could affect the government's ability to resolve the issue.
3. Answers will vary, but students should indicate ways candidates might try to take advantage of voter behavior, such as by appealing to personal views.

SECTION 1
Taking Notes
Possible responses for "Factor" column: family, school, work, age, race, gender, religion, and mass media. Possible responses for the "How it shapes public opinion" column

should give one or two details explaining why each factor is important.

Section Summary
1. By voting for a person whose beliefs and positions you support, you share your personal beliefs and positions.
2. Possible responses: Family, school, work, age, race, gender, religion.
3. A person can better avoid propaganda by accessing news through more than one source.
4. A sample gives pollsters a look at how the bigger group the sample represents feels about an issue.

SECTION 2
Taking Notes
Possible responses for "Types of interest groups": agricultural groups, business groups, labor groups, professional groups, societal groups, and cause-based groups.

Section Summary
1. By organizing as a large group, members are more likely to reach politicians and other parts of the public with their message.
2. Cause-based interest groups represent a cause or issue, rather than a group within the U.S. population.
3. Advantage: The groups represent minority interests. Disadvantages: The groups can have too much influence, rely on emotional appeals, and prevent Congress from acting.

SECTION 3
Taking Notes
Possible responses for "How parties serve the public good": filter out extreme ideas, provide political and social stability, discourage short-term shifts in power, and provide a "brand name" for voters who do not know candidates well

Section Summary
1. After elections, parties continue to monitor their candidates' behavior. Elected party

members also tend to organize power by party membership.
2. All parties compete in a multiparty system, unless they join to form a majority. In a two-party system, it is very difficult for additional parties to compete with the two major parties.
3. No. State and national party committees also support local candidates.
4. Answers will vary, but students should paraphrase three of the five benefits listed.

SECTION 4
Taking Notes
Possible responses for "Factors that influence voter behavior": party identification, the voter's own views, a candidate's personal and professional background, and the voter's background.

Section Summary
1. Hard money is contributed directly to the candidate, while soft money is donated to the candidate's party.
2. No; in a closed primary, voters can only vote for a candidate running for the party in which the voter is registered.
3. Too many people may believe that their vote does not make a difference, and registration may be too difficult.
4. No; if more than two candidates are running, one candidate can win a race with a plurality of votes that is smaller than what a majority of votes would be.

Chapter 10: Civil Liberties
CHAPTER SUMMARY
1. liberties and rights, fundamental freedoms
2. Answers will vary but students may mention the importance of protecting the rights of all Americans.
3. Answers will vary but students should discuss one of the five freedoms mentioned and explain why it is fundamental.

Teacher Management System

SECTION 1

Taking Notes

Possible responses for how the Bill of Rights protects Americans' civil liberties should note how the Bill of Rights protects civil liberties and civil rights, as well as how these protections can be limited and have been applied to state governments.

Section Summary

1. No. While the Bill of Rights lists specific rights, it also does not deny the existence of other rights.
2. when the person's actions harm another person or conflict with civic responsibilities
3. to explain and justify the Supreme Court's decisions to merge some of the Bill of Rights with the Fourteenth Amendment

SECTION 2

Taking Notes

Possible responses for "First Amendment Freedoms": freedoms of religion, freedoms of speech, freedoms of the press, freedoms of assembly, and freedoms of petition

Section Summary

1. an official religion or government support for one religion over another
2. Possible answer: It allows Americans to contact or criticize politicians for almost any reason, plus it allows Americans to watch and listen to most government actions and read many government documents.
3. Answers will vary, but students should discuss how it involves government attempts to stop future publication of certain information.
4. It can restrict when, where, and how some assemblies are held.

SECTION 3

Taking Notes

Possible responses for Second Amendment: protects the right to form a militia and bear arms; possible responses for Third Amendment: prevents the government from forcing its citizens to house troops; possible

responses for Fourth Amendment: prevents the government from searching a building or seizing a person without probable cause or legal authority; possible response for Fifth Amendment: protects people accused of a crime

Section Summary

1. to allow states to form their own militias and to relieve Americans' fears of an overly powerful, federally-controlled standing army
2. the use of evidence obtained illegally against a person
3. Possible answers: through Supreme Court decisions; interpretation of certain amendments
4. Procedural due process involves government procedures; substantive due process involves the laws used to punish a person.

SECTION 4

Taking Notes

Responses will vary, but students should list in the first column the rights of people accused of crimes, such as the right to not incriminate oneself, the right to a speedy and public trial, and the right to protection from cruel and unusual punishment. Students should give details for each right in the second column.

Section Summary

1. Possible answers: trial, mediation, arbitration, negotiation
2. trial
3. their constitutional rights as an accused person
4. No. In a bench trial, only a judge hears and decides the case.

Chapter 11: Civil Rights

CHAPTER SUMMARY

1. Legislation banning discrimination based on a variety of factors was passed.
2. Answers will vary, but students may discuss how the concept of equality defines what the United States and its government stands for.
3. Answers will vary, but students should explain how people needed to see everyone as equal before they could treat them the same under the law.

SECTION 1

Taking Notes

Possible responses for the "Civil Rights" column should identify and describe specific civil rights and what they; possible responses for the "Discrimination" column should tell how discrimination has affected different groups in the United States

Section Summary

1. the Constitution and its amendments, federal and state laws, and Supreme Court decisions
2. States continued to pass discriminatory laws.
3. Answers will vary, but students may discuss how many Japanese Americans were forced to relocate because of their ethnic background.

SECTION 2

Taking Notes

Possible response for "Equal Protection": a clause in the Fourteenth Amendment that requires states to apply the law the same way for all people; Possible responses for "African Americans" should address historical events and details related to how the equal protection clause was unevenly applied and gradually extended to African Americans, such as segregation, Jim Crow laws, the separate but equal doctrine, desegregation, and de facto segregation, and *Brown* v. *Board of Education of Topeka, Kansas*; possible responses for

"Women" should note how women worked for equal rights and suffrage.

Section Summary

1. unequal treatment in the same legal situation
2. No, it only gave African American men the right to vote.
3. state level
4. De jure segregation is segregation as a result of law; de facto segregation is segregation as a result of fact, not law.

SECTION 3

Taking Notes

Possible responses for "Civil Rights Movement" should provide details about the civil rights movement, such as acts of civil disobedience; possible responses for "Civil Rights Laws" should provide details about specific civil rights legislation, such as the Civil Rights Act of 1964, and the effects of civil rights laws.

Section Summary

1. Possible answers: boycotts, sit-ins, marches
2. discrimination based on race, color, religion, sex, national origin
3. bans gender-based discrimination and sexual harassment; right to equal pay; right to an abortion
4. Possible answer: Affirmative action gave special opportunities to certain groups, and some members of the majority felt discriminated against.

SECTION 4

Taking Notes

Possible responses for "Citizenship" should explain how a person becomes a citizen, as well as what is expected of citizens; possible responses for "Immigration" should note how immigration—including illegal immigration—has been experienced in the United States.

Section Summary

1. A naturalized citizen was not born to American parents, as under jus soli. He or

Teacher Management System

she would have gone through the process of naturalization to become a citizen.

2. Possible answers: voting, respecting laws and others' rights, paying taxes

3. The government began to more closely regulate immigration, barring entry to certain groups of immigrants.

4. Against: Illegal immigrants take jobs away from Americans. For: Illegal immigrants are just trying to build a better life for themselves.

Chapter 12: Understanding Elections

CHAPTER SUMMARY

1. educate themselves, vote, work on campaigns, run for office

2. Answers will vary but students may say that candidates are able to reach more and different types of voters through different media outlets.

3. Possible answer: Since a republic is a government in which the people hold political power, voting is the most basic way people can express their beliefs and maintain this power.

SECTION 1
Taking Notes

Answers will vary, but student responses should show an understanding of the most important points of the section.

Section Summary

1. so that the public can know where he or she stands on certain issues

2. how the part of the population they represent feels about a candidate and his or her platform

3. states with several electoral votes, states where support for opponents is weak, or swing states

4. If used incorrectly, sound bites can negatively affect a candidate's campaign.

SECTION 2
Taking Notes

Answers will vary, but student responses should show an understanding of the most important points of the section.

Section Summary

1. Traficant used donations for personal use. DeLay helped transfer national corporate donations to campaigns in a state where corporations cannot donate to state candidates.

2. individual donations

3. Unlike an individual donation, soft money is a donation *not* directly given to a candidate.

4. that PACs will have undue influence on officeholders

5. The candidate must appear in the ad, along with audio of the candidate indicating that he or she approves of the message.

SECTION 3
Taking Notes

Answers will vary, but student responses should show an understanding of the most important points of the section.

Section Summary

1. They felt that the machines used for the first recount could not accurately read all of the ballots.

2. Older voters are more likely to vote than younger voters.

3. their experience, background, and stance on major issues

4. to make sure federal and state representatives represent about the same number of people

5. Possible answers: phone voters on election day to ask for support, offer rides to the polls, target people who have not voted yet

Chapter 13: Supreme Court Cases

CHAPTER SUMMARY
1. holding, exploring, exchanging, expressing, and debating ideas
2. Answers will vary. Possible answer: so that state governments and the federal governments did not regulate the same type of commerce in different ways
3. Answers will vary, but students should discuss what might happen *without* the protections of both due process and equal protection.

SECTION 1
Taking Notes
Answers will vary, but student responses should show an understanding of the most important points of the section.

Section Summary
1. If student expression does not strongly interfere with everyday school operations, it should be allowed.
2. First Amendment
3. express their beliefs however they want
4. political speech, vulgar and obscene speech
5. when they are held on public property

SECTION 2
Taking Notes
Answers will vary, but student responses should show an understanding of the most important points of the section.

Section Summary
1. It ruled that the use of a drug-sniffing dog at a routine traffic stop was a violation of Caballes's Fourth Amendment rights.
2. Possible answer: Government officials look for evidence in a search, and keep it in a seizure.
3. No. For the plain-view doctrine to apply, the drugs would have to be out in the open, in plain sight.

4. the special needs test: a person's legal status, the invasiveness of the search, and whether the search served some safety or security need for society
5. certain government agencies; not judges

SECTION 3
Taking Notes
Answers will vary, but student responses should show an understanding of the most important points of the section.

Section Summary
1. He was not allowed a hearing before or after his suspension.
2. It ensures that all Americans are treated exactly the same way under the law.
3. It interfered with employers' and employees' rights to make contracts—a property right.
4. It established that every American is entitled to at least a formal notice and hearing before the government can deprive him or her of rights or property.
5. Answers will vary. Possible answer: The court violated the equal-opportunity clause by treating Gault differently than an adult defendant. It also violated the due-process clause by not giving his family a chance to testify, not swearing in witnesses, not recording the hearing, and not giving Gault the chance to confront his offender.

SECTION 4
Taking Notes
Answers will vary, but student responses should show an understanding of the most important points of the section.

Section Summary
1. the passage of a related treaty between the United States and Great Britain
2. Possible answer: by assigning different regulatory powers to the federal government and state governments
3. when it does not require national, uniform regulation
4. Attorneys for the federal government argued that guns in school zones could lead to violent crime and interrupt

students' learning, both outcomes that could affect the economy.

5. In *Gonzales* v. *Raich*, the Court declared the application of the commerce clause constitutional.

Chapter 14: Making Foreign Policy

CHAPTER SUMMARY

1. protect national security, establish free and open trade, promote world peace, support democracy, provide aid to people in need

2. Possible answer: By promoting international cooperation, UN member nations can help preempt conflicts between nations.

3. Answers will vary, but students should discuss how policymakers are affected by the opinions of their constituents.

SECTION 1
Taking Notes

Answers will vary, but student responses should show an understanding of the most important points of the section.

Section Summary

1. the Hutus, the country's largest ethnic group

2. The internationalist approach promotes interaction with other countries, while the isolationist approach promotes avoiding most interaction.

3. Maintaining healthy relationships with other nations helps the United States avoid conflicts.

4. to pressure a government to make changes by preventing transactions that are key to that nation's economy

5. just peace

SECTION 2
Taking Notes

Answers will vary, but student responses should show an understanding of the most important points of the section.

Section Summary

1. their struggle with Fidel Castro and Cuba's communist government

2. Department of State employees who work overseas

3. to collect and analyze information about other nations

4. The War Powers Act of 1973 mandates that the president work closely with Congress after committing troops.

5. They hope to influence legislation.

SECTION 3
Taking Notes

Answers will vary, but student responses should show an understanding of the most important points of the section.

Section Summary

1. The critics thought President Bush should have made his decision to attack with other U.N. member nations.

2. Answers will vary, but students should paraphrase the four goals listed in the UN charter: international peace and security; friendly relations among nations; international cooperation in solving economic, social, cultural, and humanitarian problems; center for harmonizing members actions.

3. Votes by the Security Council hold authority.

4. General Assembly, Security Council, Economic and Social Council, International Court of Justice, Trusteeship Council, Secretariat

5. people in developing nations

SECTION 4
Taking Notes

Answers will vary, but student responses should show an understanding of the most important points of the section.

Section Summary

1. that they could have the civil and political rights that they deserved

2. The United States was isolationist and remained neutral during European conflicts.

3. prevent the further spread of communism
4. the fact that most Middle Eastern countries do not have democratic governments, the U.S.-Israel alliance, the U.S. invasions of Afghanistan and Iraq
5. Possible answers: help maintain an adequate food supply, develop literacy and equal access to education, eradicate malaria, tuberculosis, and HIV/AIDS

Chapter 15: Comparative Political and Economic Systems

CHAPTER SUMMARY

1. an economy in which elements of traditional, market, and command economies are combined
2. Possible answer: fair, respectful
3. Answers will vary, but students should discuss how a government of one cannot represent the needs of all groups and how citizens need to be able to choose from a variety of potential leaders in order to find those who will listen to and help them.

SECTION 1
Taking Notes
Answers will vary, but student responses should show an understanding of the most important points of the section.

Section Summary
1. gain the people's trust, partially by conducting free, open, and fair elections
2. Three-fifths of the seats in the bicameral legislature are elected and the rest are distributed in proportion to parties' share of the popular vote.
3. It chooses and can remove the chief executive.
4. There are many political parties in Parliament and coalitions help politicians put aside at least some of their differences to work together
5. It has established a democracy and elected a president.

SECTION 2
Taking Notes
Answers will vary, but student responses should show an understanding of the most important points of the section.

Section Summary
1. It is isolated from the rest of the world and rarely receives foreign aid.
2. Citizens' civil and human rights are rarely or never protected; rulers may use force to squelch opposition; governments not limited by existing law.
3. Answers will vary, but students should discuss the hierarchy of the CPSU, Central Committee, and Politburo.
4. No. Although members are elected by the people, they mainly carry out State Council and CCP decisions.
5. Benito Mussolini (Italy) and Adolf Hitler (Germany)

SECTION 3
Taking Notes
Answers will vary, but student responses should show an understanding of the most important points of the section.

Section Summary
1. made the transition to an economy based on free markets
2. Along with businesses, individuals make most economic decisions.
3. Argument for socialism: fix inequalities caused by capitalism; arguments against socialism: leads to high taxes and discourages hard work and creativity
4. It can result in poor product quality and shortages of consumer goods.

Chapter 16: State and Local Government

CHAPTER SUMMARY
1. between three branches
2. Possible answer: If citizens actively monitor and voice their opinions on local services, they are more likely to receive the services in the manner they prefer.

3. Answers will vary, but students should discuss how the model of power distribution in the federal government and other federal features lend themselves well to democracy as a whole, and therefore lower levels of government.

SECTION 1
Taking Notes
Answers will vary, but student responses should show an understanding of the most important points of the section.

Section Summary
1. South Carolinians thought that the tariff favored northern states at the expense of southern states.
2. Possible answer: It shows that the Framers accurately predicted that there would be disputes over power between the national and state government and therefore a need for a way to settle them.
3. All state constitutions express basic civic principles and practices, include a bill of rights, limit government, and divide power among three branches of government.
4. Statutory laws is often obsolete and makes for an overly long constitution.

SECTION 2
Taking Notes
Answers will vary, but student responses should show an understanding of the most important points of the section.

Section Summary
1. It made it stricter, mandating driver education in some cases and supervised driving.
2. Possible answers: power is divided among three branches; legislatures are usually bicameral, with a House of Representatives and a Senate; there is a chief executive; there are both trial and appellate courts
3. Citizen legislatures meet only once every other year and for a period of about two months, whereas professional legislatures may be held annually and last for much of the year.

4. to allow the governor to reject certain parts of legislation but sign the rest into law
5. Possible answer: A nonpartisan commission compiles a list of candidates, then the governor appoints a judge using that list. In the next election, voters can choose to keep the judge or vote him or her out of office.

SECTION 3
Taking Notes
Answers will vary, but student responses should show an understanding of the most important points of the section.

Section Summary
1. The town government issued a moratorium on construction, then held hearings and commissioned a study to determine answers to residents' concerns.
2. Possible answer: municipal government, since it would be more familiar with local issues and potentially more accessible to citizens
3. to regulate land use
4. propose and potentially have a law passed and enacted

Spanish/English
Interactive Reader
and Study Guide

SPANISH/ENGLISH INTERACTIVE READER AND STUDY GUIDE

The *Spanish/English Interactive Reader and Study Guide* is a bilingual tool for helping Spanish-speaking students who need additional support in order to grasp the concepts presented in *Holt McDougal United States Government: Principles in Practice*.

For each section, the *Spanish/English Interactive Reader and Study Guide* provides the Main Idea, Key Terms, a Section Summary graphic organizer, a detailed summary, and the Section Assessment questions. The content is organized so that small chunks, or sections, are provided in both English and Spanish for easy translation.

In the side margin of each page of the Section Summary are questions and activities designed to help students interact with the text in order to better recall the information they have read. Section Assessment questions measure students' recall of a section and can be helpful in determining which students may need additional support.

The *Spanish/English Interactive Reader and Study Guide* can help you ensure that all of your students master the information covered in *Holt McDougal United States Government: Principles in Practice*. You can also use the questions to review material with the class as a whole, or as a starting point for class discussion on issues raised in the chapter.

Answers to each of the questions in the *Spanish/English Interactive Reader and Study Guide* are provided in the Answer Key that follows.

Teacher Management System

Chapter 1: Foundations of Government

English
SECTION 1
Taking Notes

Students should fill in the five circles with the following: ensure national security, maintain order, resolve conflict, provide services, and provide for the public good.

Section Summary

1. Answers will vary. Possible answers: passing legislation to fund education; improving relations with a foreign country.
2. Government is also expected to enforce laws and punish those who do not follow them.
3. Answers will vary. Possible answers: building roads, providing public housing.
4. People collectively agreed to submit to the authority of the state.

SECTION 2
Taking Notes

In the 'Form" column, students should list the government structures described in the summary, similar to the list on p. 15 in the Student Edition. In the "Details" column, students should provide at least two details about each form, similar to those found on p. 15 in the Student Edition.

Section Summary

1. The monarch is more powerful in an absolute monarchy.
2. In a direct democracy, the people make political decisions themselves. In a republic, the people elect representatives to make these decisions for them.
3. In a federal system, regional governments share power with the national government. In a confederal system, the regional governments are much more powerful than the national government.
4. Since the legislature and the prime minister are part of the same, single branch of government and are not subject to separation of powers, they do not always need the agreement of the other to get things done.

SECTION 3
Taking Notes

Students should write the three ideals at the heart of American democracy in the first rectangle. In the second rectangle, they should write the five principles of American democracy. In the third rectangle, they should write a brief explanation of how free enterprise is connected to American democracy.

Section Summary

1. Freedom of speech allows people to say what they want, as long as it does not hurt others.
2. Answers will vary, but should discuss the equal treatment of all people under the law.
3. By protecting the liberties and equality of those not in the majority, liberal democracy protects two of the three ideals central to American democracy.
4. Answers will vary. Possible response: because competition can develop more easily if the government does not too closely regulate producers.

Spanish
SECCIÓN 1
Tomar notas

Los estudiantes deben completar los cinco círculos con lo siguiente: garantizar la seguridad nacional, mantener el orden, resolver los conflictos, proveer servicios y procurar el bien común.

Resumen de la sección

1. Las respuestas variarán. Respuestas posibles: aprobar legislación para financiar la educación, mejorar las relaciones con un país extranjero

2. También se espera del gobierno que haga cumplir las leyes y que castigue a aquellos que no las cumplen.

3. Las respuestas variarán. Respuestas posibles: construir caminos, proveer viviendas

4. El pueblo acordó en forma colectiva someterse a la autoridad del estado.

SECCIÓN 2
Tomar notas

En la columna "Forma", los estudiantes deben enumerar las estructuras de gobierno que se describen en el resumen, en forma similar a las de la lista de la pág. 15 del libro del estudiante. En la columna "Detalles" los estudiantes deben dar por lo menos dos detalles acerca de cada forma, en forma similar a los que se encuentran en la pág. 15 del Edición del estudiante.

Resumen de la sección

1. El monarca tiene más poder en una monarquía absoluta.

2. En una democracia directa, el pueblo toma decisiones políticas por sí mismo. En una república, el pueblo elige representantes para que tomen las decisiones por él.

3. En un sistema federal, los gobiernos regionales comparten el poder con el gobierno nacional. En un sistema confederal, los gobiernos regionales tienen mucho más poder que el gobierno nacional.

4. Como la legislatura y el primer ministro forman parte de una misma y única rama de gobierno y no están sujetos a la separación de poderes, no siempre necesitan contar con el acuerdo del otro para tomar medidas.

SECCIÓN 3
Tomar notas

Los estudiantes deben escribir los tres ideales esenciales de la democracia estadounidense en el primer rectángulo. En el segundo rectángulo deben escribir los cinco principios de la democracia estadounidense. En el tercer rectángulo deben escribir una breve

explicación acerca de cómo se relaciona la libre empresa con la democracia estadounidense.

Resumen de la sección

1. La libertad de expresión permite que las personas digan lo que quieran siempre y cuando no lastimen a otros.

2. Las respuestas variarán, pero deben comentar acerca del tratamiento igualitario de todas las personas ante la ley.

3. Al proteger las libertades y el derecho a la igualdad de aquellos que no forman parte de la mayoría, la democracia liberal protege dos de los tres ideales centrales de la democracia estadounidense.

4. Las respuestas variarán. Respuesta posible: porque la competencia puede desarrollarse más fácilmente si el gobierno no es demasiado estricto al regular a los productores

Chapter 2: Origins of American Government
English
SECTION 1
Taking Notes

Answers will vary, but students should discuss ideas that were part of the colonists' heritage and knowledge, such as representative government and republicanism, in the left column, and events involving these ideas, such as the passage of the Fundamental Orders of Connecticut, in the right column.

Section Summary

1. representative government, individual rights, limited government

2. Possible answer: Royal colonies had less independence. Not all members of the legislature were elected by the colonists, as in a charter colony, and the colony was directly controlled by the king through a governor, unlike in a charter colony, where colonists had a say in the charter.

3. ideas such as natural rights and economic and civil liberties

SECTION 2
Taking Notes
Answers will vary, but students should list at least three causes of the American Revolution, such as the Intolerable Acts, in the left box, and three effects of the war, such as the colonists gained their independence from Great Britain, in the right box.

Section Summary
1. to help member colonies defend themselves against Native Americans and nearby Dutch colonies
2. Possible answer: Since they did not have representation in Parliament, they did not feel that Parliament had the right to tax them.
3. war and independence
4. legislatures of elected representatives, as well as judicial and executive branches, and legislative and executive branches with limited powers; many also included bills of rights

SECTION 3
Taking Notes
Answers will vary, but students should list advantages of the Articles, allowed Congress to organize the western lands, in the left column and disadvantages of the Articles, such as national government could not raise money or help defend the country, in the right column.

Section Summary
1. when at least nine states had approved it
2. No. It did not have power to raise money, and the states did not contribute much.
3. Shays's Rebellion

SECTION 4
Taking Notes
Answers will vary, but students should discuss in the different circles the various plans and compromises reached during the Constitutional Convention, such as the Virginia and New Jersey Plans, the Great Compromise, and the Three-Fifths Compromise.

Section Summary
1. No. Each state received one vote.
2. how the population of a state would affect its membership in the national legislature
3. Three-fifths of the enslaved people in a state would be counted when determining a state's population.
4. They thought that the Constitution should include a bill of rights.

SECTION 5
Taking Notes
Answers will vary, but students should discuss in the different circles the groups and decisions that affected ratification, such as the Federalists, the Antifederalists, and the decision to include a bill of rights.

Section Summary
1. They claimed that the national government proposed by the Constitution would become too strong. They also criticized the absence of a bill of rights.
2. to defend the Constitution
3. as a series of amendments proposed by Congress and ratified by the states

Spanish
SECCIÓN 1
Tomar notas
Las respuestas variarán, pero los estudiantes deben comentar en la columna izquierda las ideas que formaron parte de la herencia y los conocimientos de los colonos, como el gobierno representativo y el republicanismo, y en la columna derecha, los sucesos que tuvieron que ver con estas ideas, como la aprobación de las Órdenes Fundamentales de Connecticut.

Resumen de la sección
1. las ideas del gobierno representativo, los derechos individuales, el gobierno limitado
2. Respuesta posible: Las colonias reales tenían menos independencia. Los colonos no elegían a todos los miembros de la legislatura, como en la colonia por fueros, y el rey controlaba la colonia directamente

Teacher Management System

a través de un gobernador, a diferencia de
la colonia por fueros, donde los colonos
tenían voz y voto.
3. las ideas tales como los derechos naturales
y las libertades civiles y económicas

SECCIÓN 2
Tomar notas
Las respuestas variarán, pero los estudiantes
deben enumerar por lo menos tres causas de la
Guerra de Independencia de Estados Unidos
en el casillero de la izquierda, como por
ejemplo, las Leyes Intolerables, y tres efectos
de la guerra en el casillero de la derecha, como
por ejemplo, que los colonos lograron
independizarse de Gran Bretaña.

Resumen de la sección
1. ayudar a las colonias miembro a
defenderse de los indígenas americanos y
de las vecinas colonias holandesas
2. Respuesta posible: Como no tenían
representación en el Parlamento, creían
que el Parlamento no tenía el derecho de
cobrarles impuestos.
3. para la guerra y la independencia
4. legislaturas compuestas por representantes
electos, también las ramas judicial y
ejecutiva y las ramas legislativa y
ejecutiva con poderes limitados; muchas
también incluían declaraciones de
derechos.

SECCIÓN 3
Tomar notas
Las respuestas variarán, pero los estudiantes
deben enumerar en la columna izquierda las
ventajas de los Artículos, como por ejemplo,
que permitían al Congreso organizar los
territorios del oeste, y en la columna derecha,
las desventajas de los Artículos, como por
ejemplo, que el gobierno nacional no podía
recaudar dinero ni ayudar a defender el país.

Resumen de la sección
1. cuando fuera aprobada por al menos nueve
estados
2. No. No tenía el poder de recaudar dinero,
y los estados no contribuían demasiado.
3. la Rebelión de Shays

SECCIÓN 4
Tomar notas
Las respuestas variarán, pero los estudiantes
deben indicar en los distintos círculos los
diversos planes y compromisos alcanzados
durante la Convención Constitucional, como
los planes de Virginia y Nueva Jersey, el Gran
Compromiso y el Compromiso de los tres
quintos.

Resumen de la sección
1. No. Cada estado recibió un voto.
2. de qué manera la población de un estado
afectaría su participación en la legislatura
nacional
3. Al determinar la población de un estado se
contarían tres quintos de las personas
esclavizadas en ese estado.
4. Pensaban que la Constitución debía incluir
una declaración de derechos.

SECCIÓN 5
Tomar notas
Las respuestas variarán, pero los estudiantes
deben indicar en los distintos círculos los
grupos y las decisiones que afectaron la
ratificación, como los federalistas, los
antifederalistas y la decisión de incluir una
declaración de derechos.

Resumen de la sección
1. Alegaban que el gobierno nacional
propuesto por la Constitución sería
demasiado fuerte. También criticaban la
ausencia de una declaración de derechos.
2. defender la Constitución
3. como una serie de enmiendas propuestas
por el Congreso y ratificadas por los
estados

Chapter 3: The Constitution

English
SECTION 1
Taking Notes
Students should fill in the six circles with the
following phrases: popular sovereignty,
limited government, separation of powers,

checks and balances, judicial review, and federalism.

Section Summary

1. They were worried that citizens' rights would be suppressed.
2. By voting for who should represent them, people are choosing who should make up the government.
3. The Framers felt that government officials would not misuse their power if they had to follow the same laws as everyone else.
4. The judicial branch can declare legislation unconstitutional. The legislative branch can override vetoes.
5. The Tenth Amendment was necessary to fairly define which powers belonged to the national government and which powers belonged to the state governments.

SECTION 2
Taking Notes

Answer will vary. Possible answers in "Proposing" column: proposing amendment always requires supermajority; ratifying amendment always requires supermajority and action by state legislatures. Possible answers in "Ratifying" column: proposing amendment can take place only in Congress or at convention involving delegates not in Congress; ratifying amendment can take places inside or outside state legislatures.

Section Summary

1. Answers will vary. Possible answers: Jefferson: forward-thinking; Madison: cautious.
2. An amendment can be proposed by at least two-thirds of each house of Congress or by a national convention called by at least two-thirds of state legislatures; it can be ratified by three-fourths of state legislatures or a convention of at least three-fourths of the states.
3. Once ratified, an amendment becomes an official, permanent part of the Constitution. Therefore, it needs to be amended just like any other part of the Constitution.

4. Answers will vary. Possible answer: amendment that changes voting laws shows how certain groups of Americans have demanded and received fair treatment under the law.

SECTION 3
Taking Notes

Answers will vary. Possible answers: Congress and the president interpret and therefore expand reach of Constitution; Federal courts use judicial review to apply Constitution to modern-day developments; Political parties and various customs have gradually affected the government structure that the Constitution describes.

Section Summary

1. Congress has interpreted the Constitution to expand the lower level of the judicial branch; the Supreme Court has interpreted the Constitution in order to make powerful decisions on the constitutionality of laws.
2. Answers will vary. Possible answer: When the constitutionality of a law is being debated, people on either side of the debate may interpret parts of the Constitution differently.
3. Answers will vary. Possible answer: A political party helps a candidate get elected; if he or she wins, the candidate is then probably expected to help put the party's political agenda into place.
4. People believe that states with large populations should be assigned more senators than states with smaller populations.

Spanish
SECCIÓN 1
Tomar notas

Los estudiantes deben completar los seis círculos con las siguientes frases: soberanía popular, gobierno limitado, separación de poderes, equilibrio de poderes, recurso de inconstitucionalidad y federalismo.

Resumen de la sección

1. Les preocupaba que se suprimieran los derechos de los ciudadanos.
2. Al votar a la persona que los representará, las personas eligen quién formará parte del gobierno.
3. Los redactores pensaron que, si los funcionarios de gobierno tenían que respetar las mismas leyes que el resto de las personas, no abusarían de su poder.
4. La rama judicial puede declarar que una legislación es inconstitucional. La rama legislativa puede anular vetos.
5. La Décima Enmienda fue necesaria para definir qué poderes pertenecían al gobierno nacional y qué poderes pertenecían a los gobiernos estatales.

SECCIÓN 2

Tomar notas

Las respuestas variarán. Respuesta posible en la columna de "Proponer": Para proponer una enmienda siempre se necesita una mayoría calificada y que actúen las legislaturas estatales. Respuesta posible en la columna de "Ratificar": Sólo se puede proponer una enmienda en el Congreso o en una convención en la que se encuentren delegados ajenos al Congreso; se puede ratificar una enmienda en las legislaturas estatales o fuera de ellas.

Resumen de la sección

1. Las respuestas variarán. Respuestas posibles: Jefferson: innovador; Madison: cauteloso
2. Una enmienda puede ser propuesta por al menos dos tercios de cada cámara del Congreso o por una convención nacional convocada por, al menos, dos tercios de las asambleas legislativas estatales; puede ser ratificada por tres cuartos de las asambleas legislativas estatales o por una convención de, al menos, tres cuartos de los estados.
3. Una vez que se ratifica una enmienda, se convierte en una parte oficial y permanente de la Constitución. Por lo tanto, se debe enmendar del mismo modo

que cualquier otra parte de la Constitución.
4. Las respuestas variarán. Respuesta posible: Las enmiendas que cambian las leyes electorales muestran cómo ciertos grupos de estadounidenses han demandado y recibido un trato justo ante la ley.

SECCIÓN 3

Tomar notas

Las respuestas variarán. Respuestas posibles: El Congreso y el presidente interpretan y, por lo tanto, amplían el alcance de la Constitución; Los tribunales federales usan el recurso de inconstitucionalidad para aplicar la Constitución a situaciones actuales; los partidos políticos y algunas costumbres han afectado gradualmente a la estructura gubernamental que se describe en la Constitución.

Resumen de la sección

1. El Congreso ha interpretado la Constitución para ampliar el nivel más bajo del poder judicial; la Corte Suprema ha interpretado la Constitución para poder tomar decisiones importantes respecto de la constitucionalidad de las leyes.
2. Las respuestas variarán. Respuesta posible: Cuando se debate la constitucionalidad de una ley, las personas que tienen diferentes posiciones en el debate pueden interpretar partes de la Constitución de forma diferente.
3. Las respuestas variarán. Respuesta posible: Un partido político ayuda a un candidato a ser elegido; si gana, se espera que el candidato se ocupe de la agenda política del partido.
4. Las personas creen que a los estados con poblaciones grandes se les deberían asignar más senadores que a los estados con poblaciones menores.

Chapter 4: Federalism

English

SECTION 1

Taking Notes

Answers will vary, but students should list the various powers of the national government in the left circle, a description of the powers of the state governments in the right circle, and an explanation of concurrent and shared denied powers in the overlapping section.

Section Summary

1. They gave the states all of the powers not granted to the national government.
2. only expressed powers are specifically listed in the Constitution
3. Possible answers: national government: tax exports between states, spend money unless authorized by Congress, exercise powers reserved to the states, interfere with basic liberties; states: coin money, enter into treaties
4. discrimination by a state against a person from another state

SECTION 2

Taking Notes

Answers will vary, but students should explain dual federalism in the top box, cooperative and creative federalism in the middle box, and new federalism in the bottom box.

Section Summary

1. the Supreme Court
2. The Court ruled that the creation of the bank was a necessary and proper action to take in order to carry out the expressed powers of regulating commerce and currency.
3. Answers will vary, but students should discuss how the federal government used grants—and the threat of a lack of grants—to get states to meet federal goals.
4. to return authority to the state governments

SECTION 3

Taking Notes

Answers will vary, but students should fill in the four circles with an explanation of fiscal federalism, definitions of the various grants-in-aid, and discussion of the different issues involved in federalism today.

Section Summary

1. spending, taxing, and providing aid
2. Block grants are given for general purposes, so states can spend the money as they see fit; in contrast, federal mandates require states to spend the money in a certain way to accomplish a certain goal.
3. States would be more familiar with the problems facing the regional environment than the national government would be.

Spanish

SECCIÓN 1

Tomar notas

Las respuestas variarán, pero los estudiantes deben enumerar los diferentes poderes del gobierno nacional en el círculo de la izquierda, hacer una descripción de los poderes de los gobiernos estatales en el círculo de la derecha, y dar una explicación de los poderes concurrentes y los denegados compartidos en el sector de intersección de los círculos.

Resumen de la sección

1. Les dieron a los estados todos los poderes no otorgados al gobierno nacional.
2. Sólo los poderes expresados están específicamente mencionados en la Constitución.
3. Respuestas posibles: gobierno nacional: cobrar impuestos sobre las exportaciones entre estados, gastar dinero sin autorización del Congreso, ejercer poderes reservados a los estados, interferir con las libertades básicas; estados: acuñar dinero, firmar tratados
4. la discriminación por parte de un estado contra una persona de otro estado

---

SECCIÓN 2

Tomar notas

Las respuestas variarán, pero los estudiantes deben explicar el federalismo doble en el casillero superior, el federalismo cooperativo y el federalismo creativo en el casillero del medio y el nuevo federalismo en el casillero inferior.

Resumen de la sección

1. la Corte Suprema
2. La Corte dictaminó que la creación del banco constituía una acción necesaria y justa para llevar a cabo los poderes expresados de regular el comercio y la moneda.
3. Las respuestas variarán, pero los estudiantes deben analizar de qué manera el gobierno federal usó los fondos (y la amenaza de la falta de fondos) para lograr que los estados cumplieran con los objetivos federales.
4. devolver autoridad a los gobiernos estatales

SECCIÓN 3

Tomar notas

Las respuestas variarán, pero los estudiantes deben completar los cuatro círculos con una explicación de federalismo fiscal, definiciones de los diferentes tipos de subsidios y un análisis de los diferentes problemas que afectan al federalismo en la actualidad.

Resumen de la sección

1. gastos, recaudación de impuestos y otorgamiento de subsidios
2. Los subsidios en bloque se conceden para propósitos generales, de modo que los estados pueden usar el dinero como lo consideren necesario. Por el contrario, los mandatos federales exigen a los estados que gasten el dinero de determinada manera para un objetivo específico.
3. Los estados conocen los problemas ambientales de cada región más a fondo que el gobierno nacional.

Chapter 5: Congress: The Legislative Branch

English

SECTION 1

Taking Notes

Answers will vary, but students should note the groups that members of Congress represent in the first column, the bicameral design and apportionment process of Congress in the second column, and the various ways Congress checks the executive and judicial branches in the third column.

Section Summary

1. constituents, interest groups, country as a whole
2. to make sure that each House members represents approximately the same number of people
3. the Senate
4. Possible answer: It allows Congress to potentially punish government officials who have abused their power.

SECTION 2

Taking Notes

Answers will vary, but students should list the expressed powers of Congress in one circle, the implied powers in the second circle, the nonlegislative powers in the third circle, and the powers denied to Congress in the fourth circle.

Section Summary

1. They are not specifically listed in the Constitution, as are the expressed powers.
2. direct taxes
3. testify in a certain matter
4. Possible answers: suspend the writ of habeas corpus, pass bills of attainder, pass ex post facto laws

SECTION 3

Taking Notes

Answers will vary, but students should note membership requirements and specific powers in the first circle, an explanation of how reapportionment and gerrymandering affects the House in the second circle, the different House leaders in the third circle, and an explanation of the role and importance of House committees in the fourth circle.

Section Summary

1. must be at least 25 years old, have been a U.S. citizen for at least seven years, and live in the state he or she represents
2. every 10 years, based on the results of the census
3. Answers will vary, but students should discuss how the whip tries to sway members to vote as the party leadership wants them to vote.
4. Standing committees are permanent and select committees are usually temporary.

SECTION 4
Taking Notes

Answers will vary, but students should note membership requirements in the first circle, Senate leadership roles in the second circle, Senate committees in the third circle, and Senate rules and traditions in the fourth circle.

Section Summary

1. Elections take place every two years, when one-third of all seats are contested. The elections are open to all registered voters.
2. Senate majority leader
3. Under seniority rule, the senator who has served the longest on a committee becomes that committee's chair.
4. to prevent a vote in the Senate

SECTION 5
Taking Notes

Answers will vary, but students should note the various steps a bill goes through in the various boxes, such as referral, hearings in subcommittee, subcommittee report and recommendation, committee recommendation, and the different ways a bill is then debated, amended, and voted upon in each the House and the Senate.

Section Summary

1. to pass legislation that would never pass any other way
2. by listening to witnesses make statements on the bill
3. to reduce the quorum needed to conduct business
4. to reconcile different versions of the same bill in the House and the Senate

Spanish
SECCIÓN 1
Tomar notas

Las respuestas variarán, pero los estudiantes deben anotar los grupos que representan los miembros del Congreso en la primera columna, el diseño bicameral y el proceso de distribución de puestos del Congreso en la segunda columna y las distintas maneras en que el Congreso controla las ramas ejecutiva y judicial en la tercera columna.

Resumen de la sección

1. a los electores, los grupos de interés, el país en su totalidad
2. asegurarse de que cada miembro de la Cámara de Representantes representa aproximadamente a la misma cantidad de personas
3. el Senado
4. Respuesta posible: Permite que el Congreso pueda penalizar a funcionarios del gobierno que han abusado de su poder.

SECCIÓN 2
Tomar notas

Las respuestas variarán, pero los estudiantes deben enumerar los poderes expresados del Congreso en un círculo, los poderes implícitos del Congreso en el segundo círculo, los poderes no legislativos en el tercer círculo y los poderes denegados al Congreso en el cuarto círculo.

Resumen de la sección

1. Los poderes implícitos no están específicamente mencionados en la Constitución, como lo están los poderes expresados.

2. impuestos directos

3. testificar sobre un asunto en particular

4. Respuestas posibles: suspender la orden de hábeas corpus, aprobar leyes de extinción de derechos civiles, aprobar leyes *ex post facto*

SECCIÓN 3
Tomar notas

Las respuestas variarán, pero los estudiantes deben anotar los requisitos de membresía y los poderes específicos en el primer círculo, una explicación de cómo la redistribución y la manipulación de distritos afectan a la Cámara de Representantes en el segundo círculo, los distintos dirigentes de la Cámara de Representantes en el tercer círculo y una explicación de la función e importancia de los comités de la Cámara de Representantes en el cuarto círculo.

Resumen de la sección

1. Deben tener al menos 25 años, haber sido ciudadanos estadounidenses durante al menos siete años y vivir en el estado que representan.

2. cada 10 años, según los resultados del censo

3. Las respuestas variarán, pero los estudiantes deberían comentar cómo el coordinador trata de influir en los miembros para que voten como quieren los dirigentes del partido.

4. Los comités permanentes son estables y los comités selectos son, en general, temporales.

SECCIÓN 4
Tomar notas

Las respuestas variarán, pero los estudiantes deben anotar los requisitos de membresía en el primer círculo, las figuras de liderazgo en el Senado en el segundo círculo, los comités del Senado en el tercer círculo y las reglas y tradiciones del Senado en el cuarto círculo.

Resumen de la sección

1. Las elecciones se realizan cada dos años y se renueva un tercio de los puestos. Las elecciones están abiertas a todos los votantes inscritos.

2. el líder de la mayoría del Senado

3. Según la regla de antigüedad, el senador que ha trabajado más tiempo en un comité se convierte en el presidente del comité.

4. evitar que se realice una votación en el Senado

SECCIÓN 5
Tomar notas

Las respuestas variarán, pero los estudiantes deben anotar los diferentes pasos que atraviesa un proyecto de ley en los distintos recuadros, como remitir el proyecto de ley, las audiencias del subcomité, los informes y la recomendación del subcomité, la recomendación del comité y las diferentes formas en que luego se debate, enmienda y vota un proyecto en la Cámara de Representantes y en el Senado.

Resumen de la sección

1. para aprobar legislación que nunca se aprobaría de otro modo

2. escuchando a testigos que manifiestan opiniones sobre el proyecto de ley

3. para reducir el quórum necesario para tomar decisiones

4. para conciliar versiones diferentes del mismo proyecto de ley en la Cámara de Representantes y en el Senado

Chapter 6: The Presidency

English
SECTION 1
Taking Notes

Answers will vary. Possible answers in "Formal" column: chief executive, chief administrator, commander in chief, foreign policy leader, chief agenda setter, at least 35 years of age, lived in the country for 14 years, natural-born citizen. Possible answers in "Informal" column: chief of state, party leader, chief citizen, experience, impressive personal qualities.

Section Summary

1. chief executive, chief administrator, commander in chief, foreign policy leader, chief agenda setter
2. No, because she was born a French citizen, not a U.S. citizen.
3. Until the legislation was passed, there was no formal line of succession to follow if the president was unable to serve.
4. male, white, well-educated, Christian, usually military experience

SECTION 2
Taking Notes

Answers will vary. Possible answers in the first box: Executive Powers: appoint and remove, issue executive orders, use executive privilege. Possible answers in the second box: Diplomatic and Military Powers: negotiate treaties, make executive agreements, grant diplomatic recognition, call out armed forces. Possible answers in the third box: Legislative and Judicial Powers: propose legislation; veto legislation; nominate federal judges and justices; grant reprieves, pardons, and amnesty; commute sentences.

Section Summary

1. Executive agreements do not require Senate consent.
2. grant pardons, grant reprieves, grant amnesty, and commute sentences
3. The president can use the media to gather and maintain support.

SECTION 3
Taking Notes

Answers will vary, but students should mention the Executive Office of the President, the chief of staff, the vice president, and the cabinet.

Section Summary

1. to organize the president's many advisers and assistants and executive programs and agencies
2. to coordinate issues of national security.
3. Recently, the vice president has become more of an adviser to the president and

now sometimes manages executive projects.
4. an interpretation of part of the Constitution

Spanish
SECCIÓN 1
Tomar notas

Las respuestas variarán. Respuestas posibles en la columna "Formal": jefe del ejecutivo, jefe de gobierno, comandante en jefe, líder de la política exterior, establece la agenda del país, al menos 35 años de edad, 14 años de residencia en el país, ser ciudadano nacido en el país. Respuestas posibles en la columna "Informal": jefe de estado, líder del partido, ciudadano líder, experiencia, características personales admirables

Resumen de la sección

1. jefe del ejecutivo, jefe de gobierno, comandante en jefe, líder de la política exterior, establece la agenda del país
2. No, porque nació como ciudadana de Francia, no de Estados Unidos.
3. Hasta que se aprobó la ley, no había una línea formal de sucesión establecida en caso de que el presidente no pudiese continuar cumpliendo sus funciones.
4. hombres, blancos, con buena educación, cristianos, usualmente con experiencia militar

SECCIÓN 2
Tomar notas

Las respuestas variarán. Respuestas posibles en el primer casillero: Poderes ejecutivos: nombrar y destituir, dictar órdenes ejecutivas, hacer uso del privilegio ejecutivo. Respuestas posibles en el segundo casillero: Poderes diplomáticos y militares: negociar tratados, firmar acuerdos ejecutivos, otorgar reconocimiento diplomático, convocar a las fuerzas armadas. Respuestas posibles en el tercer casillero: Poderes legislativos y judiciales: proponer una ley, vetar un proyecto de ley, nombrar jueces y magistrados federales, otorgar conmutaciones, indultos y amnistías, conmutar sentencias

Resumen de la sección

1. Los acuerdos ejecutivos no requieren la aprobación del Senado.
2. conceder indultos, otorgar conmutaciones, ofrecer amnistías y conmutar sentencias
3. El presidente puede hacer uso de los medios de comunicación para conseguir apoyo y mantenerlo.

SECCIÓN 3
Tomar notas

Las respuestas variarán, pero los estudiantes deben mencionar la Oficina Ejecutiva del Presidente, al jefe del estado mayor, al vicepresidente y al gabinete.

Resumen de la sección

1. para organizar a la gran cantidad de asesores y asistentes del presidente y los programas y agencias ejecutivos
2. coordinar asuntos de seguridad nacional
3. En el último tiempo, el vicepresidente se ha transformado cada vez más en un asesor del presidente y en la actualidad a veces administra proyectos ejecutivos.
4. de la interpretación de una parte de la Constitución

Chapter 7: The Executive Branch at Work

English
SECTION 1
Taking Notes

Students should fill in the three circles with the following information: office of the vice president and Executive Office of the President; executive departments; independent executive agencies, independent regulatory commissions, and government corporations.

Section Summary

1. a clear, formal structure; a division of labor; and a set of rules and procedures by which it operates.
2. The president gives out executive jobs to people he or she wants to reward, instead of people who were qualified for the jobs.

3. It made it illegal to hire people for civil-service jobs based on their party affiliation.

SECTION 2
Taking Notes

Answer will vary, but students should write characteristics of independent agencies in the top circle, such as have some legislative and judicial powers and sometimes can enforce own laws, and characteristics of the executive departments in the bottom circle, such as headed by cabinet members and contain internal, specific agencies. In the area shared by the two circles, students should write common characteristics, such as created by Congress.

Section Summary

1. Congress confirms high-level position nominees within the executive departments and controls departments' duties, powers, and budgets.
2. Possible answers: Food and Drug Administration, Coast Guard, Secret Service
3. It creates a government corporation when it realizes that a private corporation would not be able to meet a national need and still make a decent profit.
4. It has passed legislation to check agencies, including settings guidelines for agency rules and making agency information available to the public.

SECTION 3
Taking Notes

Answers will vary, but students should fill in the circles with the following information: taxes, fees, nontax sources, and borrowing.

Section Summary

1. Since a proportional tax is applied the same against all income, it affects lower-income earners more than upper-income earners.
2. by selling bonds
3. the House and Senate Appropriations Committees, with the advice of other

members of Congress and the Congressional Budget Office

4. Spending money strategically and cutting taxes are both ways to stimulate the economy.

Spanish
SECCIÓN 1
Tomar notas

Los estudiantes deben completar los tres círculos con la siguiente información: oficina del vicepresidente y Oficina Ejecutiva del Presidente; departamentos ejecutivos; agencias ejecutivas independientes, comisiones reguladoras independientes y empresas públicas.

Resumen de la sección

1. una estructura formal clara; división del trabajo y un conjunto de reglas y procedimientos con los cuales opera
2. El presidente asignaba cargos ejecutivos a personas que quería recompensar, en lugar de asignarlos a personas calificadas para el empleo.
3. Declaró ilegal la contratación basada en la afiliación partidaria de personas para cargos en el funcionariado.

SECCIÓN 2
Tomar notas

Las respuestas variarán, pero los estudiantes debería escribir las características de las agencias independientes en el círculo superior, como que tienen algunos poderes legislativos y judiciales y que a veces pueden hacer cumplir leyes propias, y las características de los departamentos ejecutivos en el círculo inferior, como que están encabezados por miembros del gabinete y que comprenden agencias internas y específicas. En el área que comparten ambos círculos, los estudiantes deben escribir características en común, como que son creados por el Congreso.

Resumen de la sección

1. El Congreso confirma designaciones a cargos de alto rango dentro de los departamentos ejecutivos y controla los deberes, poderes y presupuestos de los departamentos.
2. Respuestas posibles: Administración de Drogas y Alimentos, Guardia Costera, Servicio Secreto
3. Crea una empresa pública cuando se da cuenta de que una empresa privada no podría satisfacer una necesidad nacional y al mismo tiempo obtener ganancias suficientes.
4. Ha aprobado legislación para controlar a las agencias, que incluye el establecimiento de pautas para reglamentarlas y la disponibilidad pública de la información.

SECCIÓN 3
Tomar notas

Las respuestas variarán, pero los estudiantes deben completar los círculos con la siguiente información: impuestos, tarifas, ingresos no impositivos y préstamos.

Resumen de la sección

1. Dado que un impuesto proporcional se aplica del mismo modo sobre todo el ingreso, afecta más a los grupos con ingresos bajos que a los grupos con ingresos altos.
2. vendiendo bonos
3. los Comités de asignación de fondos de la Cámara de Representantes y del Senado, con el asesoramiento de otros miembros del Congreso y de la Oficina de Presupuesto del Congreso
4. Gastar dinero estratégicamente y recortar los impuestos son dos maneras de estimular la economía.

Chapter 8: The Federal Courts and the Judicial Branch

English
SECTION 1
Taking Notes

Students should fill in the three circles with the following phrases: district courts, courts of appeal, and Supreme Court. Students should also provide at least two bullet points of information about each type of court.

Section Summary

1. They identify if a law has been broken and if penalties apply, they decide how to provide relief to those who have been harmed, and, if relevant, they determine the meaning of a specific law or part of the Constitution.
2. District courts make up the lowest tier and hear most federal criminal and civil cases. Courts of appeal make up the middle tier and hear appeals from district courts and some federal agencies. The Supreme Court makes up the highest tier and mainly hears appeals from the lower courts.
3. the judicial restraint end of the spectrum
4. the appointment process of judges, the amendment process, and the power to impeach and remove judges

SECTION 2
Taking Notes

Answers will vary. Possible answers in "District Courts" column: 94 courts, hear specific cases cited in Constitution and many criminal and civil cases. Possible answers in "Courts of Appeal" column: 13 courts, hear cases on appeal from lower courts and some federal agencies, most rulings final. Possible answers in "Other Courts" column: created by Congress, have very limited jurisdiction.

Section Summary

1. to determine whether the evidence presented to it is enough to file criminal charges
2. The U.S. attorney represents the United States in federal cases in which the country or its people are affected.
3. need to show that the original ruling was affected by a legal mistake
4. U.S. Court of Federal Claims, Foreign Intelligence Surveillance Court, U.S. Court of Appeals for the Armed Forces

SECTION 3
Taking Notes

Answers will vary. Possible answers in "History" column: developed equal power to other two branches, *Dred Scott* decision checked Congress's power. Possible answers in "Appointments" column: nominated by president and confirmed by Senate, most nominees have law background. Possible answers in "Procedures" column: writ of certiorari orders review of a lower court's decision, justices can issue majority, concurrent, and dissenting opinions.

Section Summary

1. Possible answer: The decision showed that the Supreme Court had the power to check Congress.
2. Most have a background in law and share the same political party and judicial beliefs as the nominating president.
3. information about the nominee's personal and professional background, feelings on major political issues
4. No. Only five of the nine justices need to agree in order to issue a ruling.

Spanish
SECCIÓN 1
Tomar notas

Los estudiantes deben completar los tres círculos con las siguientes frases: las cortes de distrito, las cortes de apelación y Corte Suprema. Los estudiantes también deben incluir al menos dos puntos con información acerca de cada tipo de corte.

Resumen de la sección

1. Determinan si se ha infringido una ley y, si corresponden castigos, deciden cómo compensar a aquellos que han sufrido un daño. Si corresponde, determinan el significado de alguna ley en particular o de una parte de la Constitución.
2. Las cortes de distrito conforman el nivel inferior y ven la mayoría de los casos penales y civiles federales. Las cortes de apelación conforman el nivel intermedio y escuchan apelaciones de las cortes de

distrito y de algunas agencias federales. La Corte Suprema constituye el nivel superior y ante todo escucha apelaciones de las cortes inferiores.

3. el extremo de contención judicial
4. el proceso de designación de jueces, el proceso de enmiendas y el poder para llevar a juicio político y destituir a jueces

SECCIÓN 2
Tomar notas
Las respuestas variarán. Respuestas posibles en la columna "Cortes de distrito": 94 cortes, escuchan casos específicos citados en la Constitución y muchos casos penales y civiles. Respuestas posibles en la columna "Cortes de apelación": 13 cortes, escuchan casos de apelación de cortes inferiores y de algunas agencias federales, la mayoría de las decisiones son definitivas. Respuestas posibles en "Otras cortes": creadas por el Congreso, tienen una jurisdicción muy limitada.

Resumen de la sección
1. determinar si las pruebas presentadas son suficientes para presentar cargos penales
2. El Fiscal Federal representa a Estados Unidos en casos federales en los que están afectados el país o su pueblo.
3. Debe demostrar que un error legal afectó la decisión original.
4. Corte de Demandas Federales de Estados Unidos, Tribunal de Vigilancia de Inteligencia Extranjera, Corte de Apelaciones de las Fuerzas Armadas de Estados Unidos

SECCIÓN 3
Tomar notas
Las respuestas variarán. Respuestas posibles en la columna "Historia": desarrolló poderes iguales a los de las otras dos ramas, la decisión en el caso *Dred Scott* controló el poder del Congreso. Respuestas posibles en la columna "Nombramientos": propuestos por el presidente y confirmados por el Senado, la mayoría de los candidatos tienen educación en derecho. Respuestas posibles en la columna "Procedimientos": las órdenes de revisión de

sentencia exigen la revisión de decisiones de cortes inferiores, los magistrados pueden emitir opiniones de la mayoría, concurrentes y discrepantes.

Resumen de la sección
1. Respuesta posible: La decisión demostró que la Corte Suprema tenía el poder de controlar al Congreso.
2. La mayoría tiene educación en derecho y comparte el mismo partido político y las mismas opiniones sobre jurisprudencia del presidente que los propone.
3. información acerca de los antecedentes personales y profesionales del candidato, opiniones sobre temas políticos importantes
4. No. Sólo cinco de los nueve magistrados tienen que estar de acuerdo para tomar una decisión.

Chapter 9: The Political Process

English
SECTION 1
Taking Notes
Students should fill in the "Factor" column with Family, School, Work, Age, Race, Gender, Religion, and Mass Media. They should provide one or two bullet points explaining why each factor is important in the "How it shapes public opinion" column.

Section Summary
1. By voting for a person whose beliefs and positions you support, you share your personal beliefs and positions.
2. Possible answers: Family, school, work, age, race, gender, religion.
3. A person can better avoid propaganda by accessing news through more than one source.
4. A sample gives pollsters a look at how the bigger group the sample represents feels about an issue.

SECTION 2
Taking Notes
Students should fill in the six circles with the following phrases: agricultural groups, business groups, labor groups, professional groups, societal groups, and cause-based groups.

Section Summary
1. By organizing as a large group, members are more likely to reach politicians and other parts of the public with their message.
2. Cause-based interest groups represent a cause or issue, rather than a group within the U.S. population.
3. Advantage: The groups represent minority interests. Disadvantages: The groups can have too much influence, rely on emotional appeals, and prevent Congress from acting.

SECTION 3
Taking Notes
Students should fill in the four circles with phrases similar to the following: filter out extreme ideas, provide political and social stability, discourage short-term shifts in power, provide a "brand name" for voters who do not know candidates well.

Section Summary
1. After elections, parties continue to monitor their candidates' behavior. Elected party members also tend to organize power by party membership.
2. All parties compete in a multiparty system, unless they join to form a majority. In a two-party system, it is very difficult for additional parties to compete with the two major parties.
3. No. State and national party committees also support local candidates.
4. Answers will vary, but students should paraphrase three of the five benefits listed.

SECTION 4
Taking Notes
Students should fill in the four circles with the following phrases: party identification, the

voter's own views, a candidate's personal and professional background, and the voter's background.

Section Summary
1. Hard money is contributed directly to the candidate, while soft money is donated to the candidate's party.
2. No. In a closed primary, voters can only vote for a candidate running for the party in which the voter is registered.
3. Too many people may believe that their vote does not make a difference, and registration may be too difficult.
4. No. If more than two candidates are running, one candidate can win a race with a plurality of votes that is smaller than what a majority of votes would be.

Spanish
SECCIÓN 1
Tomar notas
Los estudiantes deben completar la columna "Factor" con: familia, escuela, trabajo, edad, raza, sexo, religión y medios de comunicación masiva. Deben incluir uno o dos puntos en la columna "Cómo influye en la opinión pública" para explicar por qué cada factor es importante.

Resumen de la sección
1. Al votar por una persona cuyas creencias y posturas apoyamos, compartimos nuestras creencias y posturas personales.
2. Respuestas posibles: familia, escuela, trabajo, edad, raza, sexo, religión
3. La mejor forma de evitar la propaganda es acceder a las noticias por medio de más de una fuente de información.
4. Una muestra ofrece a los encuestadores un panorama de la opinión sobre algún tema en particular del grupo más grande que representa esa muestra.

SECCIÓN 2
Tomar notas
Los estudiantes deben completar los seis círculos con las siguientes frases: grupos agricultores, grupos de empresas, grupos

sindicales, grupos de profesionales, grupos sociales y grupos basados en una causa.

Resumen de la sección

1. Al organizarse en un grupo grande, los miembros tienen más posibilidades de llegar con sus mensajes a los políticos y otros sectores públicos.
2. Los grupos de interés basados en una causa representan una causa o asunto, más que a un grupo dentro de la población de Estados Unidos.
3. Ventaja: Los grupos representan los intereses de las minorías. Desventajas: Los grupos pueden tener demasiada influencia, apelan a las emociones e impiden que el Congreso actúe.

SECCIÓN 3
Tomar notas
Los estudiantes deben completar los cuatro círculos con frases parecidas a las siguientes: descartar las ideas extremas, brindar estabilidad política y social, desalentar los cambios en el poder a corto plazo, brindar un "nombre de marca" a los votantes que no conocen bien a los candidatos.

Resumen de la sección

1. Después de las elecciones, los partidos siguen supervisando el comportamiento de sus candidatos. Los miembros electos del partido también tienden a organizar el poder nombrando a otras personas del partido.
2. Todos los partidos compiten en un sistema multipartidario, a menos que se unan para formar una mayoría. En un sistema bipartidista es muy difícil para los otros partidos competir contra los dos partidos principales.
3. No. Los comités partidarios estatales y el nacional también apoyan a los candidatos locales.
4. Las respuestas variarán, pero los estudiantes deben parafrasear tres de los cinco beneficios enumerados.

SECCIÓN 4
Tomar notas
Los estudiantes deben completar los cuatro círculos con las siguientes frases: identificación con un partido, los puntos de vista propios del votante, los antecedentes personales y profesionales del candidato y los antecedentes del votante.

Resumen de la sección

1. El dinero duro lo recibe directamente el candidato, mientras que el dinero blando se dona al partido del candidato.
2. No. En las primarias cerradas, los votantes sólo pueden votar por un candidato del partido en el que ellos estén inscritos.
3. Hay demasiadas personas que creen que su voto no influye en el resultado final e inscribirse para una elección puede llegar a ser muy difícil.
4. No. Si se postulan más de dos candidatos, uno puede ganar con una mayoría relativa menor que lo que sería la mayoría de los votos.

Chapter 10: Civil Liberties
English
SECTION 1
Taking Notes
Answers will vary, but students should discuss the various protections within the Bill of Rights—civil liberties and civil rights—and how these protections can be limited and have been applied to state governments.

Section Summary

1. No. While the Bill of Rights lists specific rights, it also does not deny the existence of other rights.
2. when the person's actions harm another person or conflict with civic responsibilities
3. to explain and justify the Supreme Court's decisions to merge some of the Bill of Rights with the Fourteenth Amendment

Teacher Management System

SECTION 2
Taking Notes
Answers will vary, but students should list the freedoms of religion, speech, the press, assembly, and petition in the individual circles, as well as details about each freedom.

Section Summary
1. an official religion or government support for one religion over another
2. Possible answer: It allows Americans to contact or criticize politicians for almost any reason, plus it allows Americans to watch and listen to most government actions and read many government documents.
3. Answers will vary, but students should discuss how it involves government attempts to stop future publication of certain information.
4. It can restrict when, where, and how some assemblies are held.

SECTION 3
Taking Notes
Answers will vary, but students should list notes about the relevant amendment in each column, such as created to allow states to form militias in first column, forbids most housing of troops without owner's consent in second column, prohibits unreasonable search and seizure in third column, and applies due process to the federal government in the fourth column.

Section Summary
1. to allow states to form their own militias and to relieve Americans' fears of an overly powerful, federally-controlled standing army
2. the use of evidence obtained illegally against a person
3. Possible answers: through Supreme Court decisions; interpretation of certain amendments
4. Procedural due process involves government procedures; substantive due process involves the laws used to punish a person.

SECTION 4
Taking Notes
Answers will vary, but students should list related rights in each box, such as right to not incriminate self in first box, right to a speedy and public trial in second box, and right to protection from cruel and unusual punishment in third box.

Section Summary
1. Possible answers: trial, mediation, arbitration, negotiation.
2. trial
3. their constitutional rights as an accused person
4. No. In a bench trial, only a judge hears and decides the case.

Spanish
SECCIÓN 1
Tomar notas
Las respuestas variarán, pero los estudiantes deben comentar acerca de las diversas protecciones dentro de la Declaración de derechos (las libertades civiles y los derechos civiles), cómo estas protecciones se pueden limitar y cómo se han aplicado a los gobiernos estatales.

Resumen de la sección
1. No. Si bien la Declaración de derechos enumera derechos específicos, por otro lado, no niega la existencia de otros derechos.
2. cuando las acciones de la persona dañan a otra persona o entran en conflicto con las responsabilidades civiles
3. para explicar y justificar las decisiones de la Corte Suprema de combinar parte de la Declaración de derechos con la Decimocuarta enmienda

SECCIÓN 2
Tomar notas
Las respuestas variarán, pero los estudiantes deben enumerar las libertades de culto, de expresión, de prensa, de reunión y de petición en los círculos individuales, como así también detalles acerca de cada tipo de libertad.

Resumen de la sección

1. el establecimiento de una religión oficial o el apoyo del gobierno a una religión por encima de otra
2. Respuesta posible: Permite a los estadounidenses contactar o criticar a los políticos casi por casi cualquier motivo y también les permite estar informados acerca de la mayoría de las acciones del gobierno y leer muchos de los documentos del gobierno.
3. Las respuestas variarán, pero los estudiantes deben comentar cómo se relaciona con intentos del gobierno para evitar la publicación de ciertos documentos.
4. Puede restringir cuándo, dónde y cómo se realizan algunas reuniones.

SECCIÓN 3

Tomar notas

Las respuestas variarán, pero los estudiantes deben anotar datos en cada columna acerca de la enmienda correspondiente; por ejemplo, en la primera columna: creada para permitir que los estados formen milicias; en la segunda columna: prohíbe en casi todos los casos albergar tropas sin el consentimiento del dueño de la vivienda; en la tercera: prohíbe el registro y la confiscación injustificados y en la cuarta: aplica el debido proceso al gobierno federal.

Resumen de la sección

1. permitir que los estados formaran sus propias milicias y aliviar así los temores de los estadounidenses de tener un ejército permanente demasiado poderoso y controlado a nivel federal
2. el uso de pruebas obtenidas en forma ilegal en contra de una persona
3. Respuestas posibles: a través de decisiones de la Corte Suprema; por medio de la interpretación de ciertas enmiendas
4. El derecho al debido proceso tiene que ver con los procedimientos que debe seguir el gobierno; el proceso sustancial previsto tiene que ver con las leyes usadas para castigar a una persona.

SECCIÓN 4

Tomar notas

Las respuestas variarán, pero los estudiantes deben enumerar los derechos relacionados con las personas acusadas de un delito en cada casillero, como el derecho a no autoincriminarse en el primer casillero, el derecho a un juicio rápido y público en el segundo casillero y el derecho a la protección contra el castigo cruel e inusual en el tercer casillero.

Resumen de la sección

1. Respuestas posibles: juicio, mediación, arbitraje, negociación
2. el juicio
3. sus derechos constitucionales como personas acusadas
4. No. En un juicio de estrado, sólo el juez escucha y decide sobre el caso.

Chapter 11: Civil Rights

English
SECTION 1

Taking Notes

Answers will vary, but students should discuss what civil rights are and what they protect in the left box and note various instances of discrimination against different groups in the second box.

Section Summary

1. the Constitution and its amendments, federal and state laws, and Supreme Court decisions
2. The states still passed laws that discriminated against African Americans, despite the federal laws.
3. Answers will vary, but students should discuss how by being forced into relocation centers, Japanese Americans were discriminated against based on their ethnic background.

SECTION 2

Taking Notes

Answers will vary, but students should detail how equal protection works in the left box, how segregation denied equal protection to African Americans in the top-right box, and how women for equal treatment in the bottom-right box.

Section Summary

1. the treatment of people in different ways within the same legal situation
2. No. It only gave African American men the right to vote.
3. state level
4. De jure segregation is segregation as a result of law; de facto segregation is segregation as a result of fact, not law.

SECTION 3

Taking Notes

Answers will vary, but students should give details of the civil rights movement in the box, such as information about acts of civil disobedience, and details of civil rights laws in the circle, such as names of various laws—like the Civil Rights Act of 1964—and what they changed.

Section Summary

1. Possible answers: boycotts, sit-ins, marches.
2. discrimination based on race, color, religion, sex, national origin—and, by 1967, age
3. bans on discrimination based on gender and bans on sexual harassment, right to equal pay and right to an abortion
4. Answers will vary. Possible answer: Affirmative action gave special opportunities to certain groups, and some members of the majority felt discriminated against.

SECTION 4

Taking Notes

Answers will vary, but students should give discuss how a person becomes a citizen in the first box, as well as what is expected of citizens. In the second box, they should note how immigration—including illegal immigration—has been received in the United States.

Section Summary

1. A naturalized citizen was not born to American parents, as under jus soli. He or she would have gone through the process of naturalization to become a citizen.
2. Possible answers: voting, respecting laws and others' rights, paying taxes
3. The government began to more closely regulate immigration, barring entry to certain groups of immigrants.
4. Possible answer: Argument against: Illegal immigrants take jobs away from Americans. Argument in defense: Illegal immigrants are just trying to build a better life for themselves.

Spanish

SECCIÓN 1

Tomar notas

Las respuestas variarán, pero los estudiantes deben comentar en el casillero izquierdo qué son los derechos civiles y qué protegen, y anotar en el segundo casillero deben anotar diversas instancias de discriminación contra diferentes grupos.

Resumen de la sección

1. la Constitución y sus enmiendas, las leyes federales y estatales y los fallos de la Corte Suprema
2. Los estados seguían aprobando leyes que discriminaban a los afroamericanos, a pesar de las leyes federales.
3. Las respuestas variarán, pero los estudiantes deben comentar cómo se discriminó a los japoneses americanos sobre la base de su origen étnico al ubicarlos por la fuerza en los centros de reubicación.

SECCIÓN 2

Tomar notas

Las respuestas variarán, pero los estudiantes deben detallar en el casillero izquierdo, cómo funciona la igualdad de protección, en el casillero superior derecho, cómo la segregación les negó protección igualitaria a los afroamericanos y en el casillero inferior derecho, cómo las mujeres lucharon por el tratamiento igualitario.

Resumen de la sección

1. el tratamiento diferenciado de las personas dentro de la misma situación legal
2. No. Sólo le dio el derecho al voto a los hombres afroamericanos.
3. a nivel estatal
4. La segregación por ley es la segregación determinada por ley; la segregación de facto es de hecho, no es por ley.

SECCIÓN 3
Tomar notas

Las respuestas variarán, pero los estudiantes deben dar detalles del movimiento por los derechos civiles en el casillero, como información sobre actos de desobediencia civil, y detalles de las leyes de derechos civiles en el círculo, como los nombres de diversas leyes (por ejemplo, la Ley de Derechos Civiles de 1964) y el cambio que prodújeron.

Resumen de la sección

1. Respuestas posibles: boicots, sentadas, marchas
2. la discriminación basada en la raza, el color, la religión, el sexo, la nacionalidad de origen y, a partir de 1967, la edad
3. la prohibición de la discriminación basada en el sexo y la prohibición del acoso sexual, el derecho a recibir igual paga y el derecho al aborto
4. Las respuestas variarán. Respuesta posible: La acción afirmativa dio oportunidades especiales a ciertos grupos y algunos miembros de la mayoría se sintieron discriminados.

SECCIÓN 4
Tomar notas

Las respuestas variarán, pero los estudiantes deben comentar en el primer casillero cómo se hace ciudadana una persona y qué se espera de los ciudadanos. En el segundo casillero, deben anotar cómo se recibió a la inmigración (incluyendo la inmigración ilegal) en Estados Unidos.

Resumen de la sección

1. Un ciudadano naturalizado no nació de padres estadounidenses, como alguien nacido bajo el principio jus soli. La persona ha debido pasar por el proceso de naturalización para hacerse ciudadana.
2. Respuestas posibles: votar, respetar las leyes y los derechos de otros, pagar impuestos
3. El gobierno comenzó a regular la inmigración más estrictamente y prohibió la entrada a ciertos grupos de inmigrantes.
4. Respuesta posible: Argumento en contra: Los inmigrantes ilegales les quitan trabajo a los estadounidenses. Argumento en defensa: Los inmigrantes ilegales sólo intentan construir una vida mejor.

Chapter 12: Understanding Elections
English
SECTION 1
Taking Notes
Answers will vary.

Section Summary

1. so that the public can know where he or she stands on certain issues
2. how the part of the population they represent feels about a candidate and his or her platform
3. states with several electoral votes, states where support for opponents is weak, or swing states
4. If used incorrectly, sound bites can negatively affect a candidate's campaign.

SECTION 2
Taking Notes
Answers will vary.

Section Summary

1. Traficant used donations for personal use. DeLay helped transfer national corporate donations to campaigns in a state where corporations cannot donate to state candidates.
2. individual donations

3. Unlike an individual donation, soft money is a donation *not* directly given to a candidate.
4. that PACs will have undue influence on officeholders
5. The candidate must appear in the ad, along with audio of the candidate indicating that he or she approves of the message.

SECTION 3
Taking Notes
Answers will vary.

Section Summary
1. They felt that the machines used for the first recount could not accurately read all of the ballots.
2. Older voters are more likely to vote than younger voters.
3. their experience, background, and stance on major issues
4. Districts need to be redrawn when the population has changed to make sure federal and state representatives represent about the same number of people.
5. Possible answers: phone voters on election day to ask for support, offer rides to the polls, target people who have not voted yet

Spanish
SECCIÓN 1
Tomar notas
Las respuestas variarán.

Resumen de la sección
1. para que el público sepa su postura acerca de ciertos temas
2. lo que opina sobre un candidato y su plataforma electoral el sector de la población que ellos representan
3. en los estados con varios votos electorales, en los estados donde hay un apoyo débil a los oponentes y en los estados clave
4. Si no se usan correctamente, los extractos pueden afectar negativamente la campaña de un candidato.

SECCIÓN 2
Tomar notas
Las respuestas variarán.

Resumen de la sección
1. Traficant usó donaciones para fines personales. DeLay ayudó a transferir donaciones de empresas nacionales a las campañas en un estado donde las empresas no pueden donar dinero a los candidatos por los estados.
2. las donaciones personales
3. A diferencia de una donación personal, el dinero blando *no* se entrega directamente al candidato.
4. que los comités de acción política tengan una influencia excesiva sobre los titulares
5. El candidato debe aparecer en el anuncio junto con el audio del candidato indicando que aprueba el mensaje.

SECCIÓN 3
Tomar notas
Las respuestas variarán.

Resumen de la sección
1. Creían que las máquinas que se usaron para el primer recuento no podían leer con precisión todas las papeletas.
2. Los votantes mayores suelen votar más que los votantes más jóvenes.
3. la experiencia que tienen, los antecedentes y su postura sobre los asuntos más importantes
4. Los distritos deben volver a trazarse cuando la población cambia para asegurar que los representantes federales y estatales representen aproximadamente a la misma cantidad de personas.
5. Respuestas posibles: llamar por teléfono a los votantes el mismo día de la elección para pedirles su apoyo, ofrecer a los votantes viajes gratuitos a las urnas, tratar de ganar el voto de las personas que todavía no han votado

Teacher Management System

Chapter 13: Supreme Court Cases

English
SECTION 1
Taking Notes
Answers will vary.

Section Summary
1. If student expression does not strongly interfere with everyday school operations, it should be allowed.
2. First Amendment
3. express their beliefs however they want
4. when they are held on public property

SECTION 2
Taking Notes
Answers will vary.

Section Summary
1. It ruled that the use of a drug-sniffing dog at a routine traffic stop was a violation of Caballes's Fourth Amendment rights.
2. Possible answer: Government officials look for evidence in a search, and keep it in a seizure.
3. No. For the plain-view doctrine to apply, the drugs would have to be out in the open, in plain sight.
4. the special needs test: a person's legal status, the invasiveness of the search, and whether the search served some safety or security need for society
5. certain government agencies; not judges

SECTION 3
Taking Notes
Answers will vary.

Section Summary
1. He was not allowed a hearing before or after his suspension.
2. It ensures that all Americans are treated exactly the same way under the law.
3. It interfered with employers' and employees' rights to make contracts—a property right.
4. It established that every American is entitled to at least a formal notice and hearing before the government can deprive him or her of rights or property.
5. Answers will vary. Possible answer: The court violated the equal-opportunity clause by treating Gault differently than an adult defendant. It also violated the due-process clause by not giving his family a chance to testify, not swearing in witnesses, not recording the hearing, and not giving Gault the chance to confront his offender.

SECTION 4
Taking Notes
Answers will vary.

Section Summary
1. the passage of a related treaty between the United States and Great Britain
2. Possible answer: by assigning different regulatory powers to the federal government and state governments
3. when it does not require national, uniform regulation
4. Attorneys for the federal government argued that guns in school zones could lead to violent crime and interrupt students' learning, both outcomes that could affect the economy.
5. In *Gonzales* v. *Raich*, the Court declared the application of the commerce clause constitutional.

Spanish
SECCIÓN 1
Tomar notas
Las respuestas variarán.

Resumen de la sección
1. Si la expresión de los estudiantes no interfiere considerablemente con el funcionamiento diario de la escuela, debería estar permitida.
2. la Primera Enmienda
3. expresar sus creencias de cualquier modo
4. cuando se realizan en propiedad privada

Teacher Management System

SECCIÓN 2
Tomar notas
Las respuestas variarán.

Resumen de la sección
1. Dictaminó que el uso de un perro de rastreo de droga en una parada policial de rutina era una violación de los derechos de Caballes establecidos en la Cuarta Enmienda.
2. Respuesta posible: Los funcionarios de gobierno buscan pruebas en un registro y la retienen en una confiscación.
3. No. Para que se aplique la doctrina de plena vista, las drogas tendrían que estar al descubierto, a plena vista.
4. la prueba de necesidades especiales: la situación legal de una persona, qué tan invasivo es el registro y si satisface una necesidad de seguridad para la sociedad
5. determinados organismos de gobierno; no los jueces

SECCIÓN 3
Tomar notas
Las respuestas variarán.

Resumen de la sección
1. No se le permitió tener una audiencia antes o después de su suspensión.
2. Asegura que todos los estadounidenses sean tratados exactamente del mismo modo ante la ley.
3. Interfería con los derechos de empleadores y empleados de hacer contratos, un derecho a la propiedad.
4. Estableció que todo estadounidense tiene derecho al menos a una notificación formal y a una audiencia antes de que el gobierno pueda privarlo de sus derechos de propiedad.
5. Las respuestas variarán. Respuesta posible: La corte violó la cláusula de igualdad de oportunidades al tratar a Gault de forma diferente que a un acusado adulto. También violó la cláusula del debido proceso al negarle a su familia la oportunidad de testificar, de citar testigos, de grabar la audiencia y al negarle a Gault

la oportunidad de confrontar a su acusador.

SECCIÓN 4
Tomar notas
Las respuestas variarán.

Resumen de la sección
1. la firma de un tratado relacionado entre Estados Unidos y Gran Bretaña
2. Respuesta posible: Asigna diferentes poderes reguladores al gobierno federal y a los gobiernos estatales.
3. cuando no requiere regulación nacional y uniforme
4. Los abogados del gobierno federal sostenían que la posesión de armas en zonas escolares podía generar delitos violentos e interrumpir el aprendizaje de los estudiantes, dos consecuencias que podrían afectar la economía.
5. En *Gonzales* vs. *Raich*, la Corte declaró que la aplicación de la cláusula de comercio era constitucional.

Chapter 14: Making Foreign Policy

English
SECTION 1
Taking Notes
Answers will vary.

Section Summary
1. the Hutus, the country's largest ethnic group
2. The internationalist approach promotes interaction with other countries, while the isolationist approach promotes avoiding most interaction.
3. Maintaining healthy relationships with other nations helps the United States avoid conflicts.
4. to pressure a government to make changes by preventing transactions that are key to that nation's economy
5. just peace

SECTION 2
Taking Notes
Answers will vary.

Section Summary
1. their struggle with Fidel Castro and Cuba's communist government
2. Department of State employees who work overseas
3. to collect and analyze information about other nations
4. The War Powers Act of 1973 mandates that the president work closely with Congress after committing troops.
5. They hope to influence legislation.

SECTION 3
Taking Notes
Answers will vary.

Section Summary
1. The critics thought President Bush should have made his decision to attack with other U.N. member nations.
2. Answers will vary, but students should paraphrase the four goals listed in the UN charter: international peace and security; friendly relations among nations; international cooperation in solving economic, social, cultural, and humanitarian problems; center for harmonizing members actions.
3. Votes by the Security Council hold authority.
4. General Assembly, Security Council, Economic and Social Council, International Court of Justice, Trusteeship Council, Secretariat
5. people in developing nations

SECTION 4
Taking Notes
Answers will vary.

Section Summary
1. that they could have the civil and political rights that they deserved
2. The United States was isolationist and remained neutral during European conflicts.

3. prevent the further spread of communism
4. the fact that most Middle Eastern countries do not have democratic governments, the U.S.-Israel alliance, the U.S. invasions of Afghanistan and Iraq
5. Answers will vary. Possible answers: help maintain an adequate food supply, develop literacy and equal access to education, eradicate malaria, tuberculosis, and HIV/AIDS

Spanish
SECCIÓN 1
Tomar notas
Las respuestas variarán.

Resumen de la sección
1. los hutus, el grupo étnico más grande del país
2. La postura internacionalista promueve la interacción con otros países, mientras que la postura aislacionista promueve lo opuesto: evitar prácticamente toda interacción.
3. Mantener relaciones saludables con otras naciones ayuda a Estados Unidos a evitar conflictos.
4. presionar a un gobierno para que haga cambios impidiéndole hacer transacciones que son clave para la economía de esa nación.
5. una paz justa

SECCIÓN 2
Tomar notas
Las respuestas variarán.

Resumen de la sección
1. su lucha contra Fidel Castro y el gobierno comunista de Cuba
2. empleados del Departamento de Estado que trabajan en el exterior
3. reunir y analizar información sobre otras naciones
4. La Ley de Poderes de Guerra de 1973 exige que después de enviar tropas al frente de batalla, el presidente trabaje en estrecha colaboración con el Congreso.
5. Esperan influir en la legislación.

SECCIÓN 3
Tomar notas
Las respuestas variarán.

Resumen de la sección
1. Los críticos pensaban que el presidente Bush debería haber tomado su decisión de atacar en conjunto con otras naciones miembro de la ONU.
2. Las respuestas variarán, pero los estudiantes deben parafrasear los cuatro objetivos enumerados en la Carta de la ONU: la paz y seguridad internacionales, las relaciones de amistad entre naciones, la cooperación internacional en la solución de problemas económicos, sociales, culturales y humanitarios, el centro que armonice las acciones de sus miembros.
3. Los votos del Consejo de Seguridad tienen carácter de cumplimiento obligatorio.
4. La Asamblea General, el Consejo de Seguridad, el Consejo Económico y Social, la Corte Internacional de Justicia, el Consejo de Administración Fiduciaria, la Secretaría General
5. a las personas que viven en las naciones en vías de desarrollo

SECCIÓN 4
Tomar notas
Las respuestas variarán.

Resumen de la sección
1. que pudieran gozar de los derechos civiles y políticos que ellos merecían
2. Estados Unidos fue aislacionista y permaneció neutral durante los conflictos europeos.
3. evitar una mayor expansión del comunismo
4. el hecho de que la mayoría de los países de Medio Oriente no tienen gobiernos democráticos, la alianza de Estados Unidos e Israel, las invasiones estadounidenses a Afganistán e Irak
5. Las respuestas variarán. Respuestas posibles: ayudar a mantener un suministro de alimentos adecuado, fomentar el alfabetismo y el acceso igualitario a la

educación, erradicar la malaria, la tuberculosis y el VIH/SIDA

Chapter 15: Comparative Political and Economic Systems

English
SECTION 1
Taking Notes
Answers will vary.

Section Summary
1. gain the people's trust, partially by conducting free, open, and fair elections
2. Three-fifths of the seats in the bicameral legislature are elected and the rest are distributed in proportion to parties' share of the popular vote.
3. It chooses and can remove the chief executive.
4. There are many political parties in Parliament and coalitions help politicians put aside at least some of their differences to work together.
5. It has established a democracy and elected a president.

SECTION 2
Taking Notes
Answers will vary.

Section Summary
1. It is isolated from the rest of the world and rarely receives foreign aid.
2. Citizens' civil and human rights are rarely or never protected; rulers may use force to squelch opposition; governments not limited by existing law.
3. Answers will vary, but students should discuss the hierarchy of the CPSU, Central Committee, and Politburo.
4. No. Although members are elected by the people, they mainly carry out State Council and CCP decisions.
5. Benito Mussolini (Italy) and Adolf Hitler (Germany)

SECTION 3
Taking Notes
Answers will vary.

Section Summary
1. made the transition to an economy based on free markets
2. Along with businesses, individuals make most economic decisions.
3. Argument for socialism: fix inequalities caused by capitalism; arguments against socialism: leads to high taxes and discourages hard work and creativity
4. It can result in poor product quality and shortages of consumer goods.

Spanish
SECCIÓN 1
Tomar notas
Las respuestas variarán.

Resumen de la sección
1. ganar la confianza de la población, en parte al realizar elecciones libres, abiertas y justas
2. Se eligen tres quintos de los puestos en la legislatura bicameral y el resto se distribuye en forma proporcional según el voto popular que obtuvo cada partido.
3. Elige y puede destituir al jefe del ejecutivo.
4. Hay muchos partidos políticos en el Parlamento y las coaliciones ayudan a los políticos a dejar de lado al menos algunas de sus diferencias para trabajar juntos.
5. porque estableció una democracia y eligió un presidente

SECCIÓN 2
Tomar notas
Las respuestas variarán.

Resumen de la sección
1. Está aislada del resto del mundo y rara vez recibe ayuda exterior.
2. Los derechos civiles y humanos rara vez (o nunca) se protegen; los gobernantes a veces recurren a la fuerza para sofocar a la oposición; la legislación no impone límites a los gobiernos.

3. Las respuestas variarán, pero los estudiantes deben comentar la jerarquía formada por el Partido Comunista de la Unión Soviética, PCUS, el Comité Central y el Politburó.
4. No. A pesar de que a sus miembros los elige el pueblo, el Congreso ejecuta principalmente las decisiones del PCC y del Consejo de Estado.
5. Benito Mussolini (Italia) y Adolfo Hitler (Alemania)

SECCIÓN 3
Tomar notas
Las respuesta variarán.

Resumen de la sección
1. Hizo la transición hacia una economía basada en el libre mercado.
2. Los individuos son, junto con las empresas, los que toman la mayor parte de las decisiones económicas.
3. Argumento a favor del socialismo: resuelven las desigualdades ocasionadas por el capitalismo; argumentos en contra del socialismo: genera impuestos elevados y desalienta el esfuerzo en el trabajo y la creatividad
4. Puede traer como consecuencia una baja en la calidad de los productos y escasez de bienes de consumo.

Chapter 16: State and Local Government
English
SECTION 1
Taking Notes
Answers will vary.

Section Summary
1. South Carolinians thought that the tariff favored northern states at the expense of southern states.
2. Possible answer: It shows that the Framers accurately predicted that there would be disputes over power between the national and state government and therefore a need for a way to settle them.

3. All state constitutions express basic civic principles and practices, include a bill of rights, limit government, and divide power among three branches of government.
4. Statutory laws is often obsolete and makes for an overly long constitution.

SECTION 2
Taking Notes
Answers will vary.

Section Summary
1. It made it stricter, mandating driver education in some cases and supervised driving.
2. Possible answers: power is divided among three branches; legislatures are usually bicameral, with a House of Representatives and a Senate; there is a chief executive; there are both trial and appellate courts
3. Citizen legislatures meet only once every other year and for a period of about two months, whereas professional legislatures may be held annually and last for much of the year.
4. to allow the governor to reject certain parts of legislation but sign the rest into law
5. Possible answer: A nonpartisan commission compiles a list of candidates, then the governor appoints a judge using that list. In the next election, voters can choose to keep the judge or vote him or her out of office.

SECTION 3
Taking Notes
Answers will vary.

Section Summary
1. The town government issued a moratorium on construction, then held hearings and commissioned a study to determine answers to residents' concerns.
2. Possible answer: municipal government, since it would be more familiar with local issues and potentially more accessible to citizens
3. to regulate land use

4. propose and potentially have a law passed and enacted

Spanish
SECCIÓN 1
Tomar notas
Las respuestas variarán.

Resumen de la sección
1. Los habitantes de Carolina del Sur pensaban que el arancel favorecía a los estados del norte a expensas de los estados del sur.
2. Respuesta posible: Demuestra que los redactores predijeron acertadamente que habría disputas por el poder entre el gobierno nacional y el estatal y que entonces existía la necesidad de contar con una forma de resolverlas.
3. Todas las constituciones estatales expresan prácticas civiles y principios básicos, incluyen una declaración de derechos, limitan al gobierno y dividen el poder entre las tres ramas de gobierno.
4. Las leyes legisladas son a menudo obsoletas y hacen que la constitución sea extremadamente larga.

SECCIÓN 2
Tomar notas
Las respuestas variarán.

Resumen de la sección
1. Lo hizo más riguroso, exigiendo en algunos casos clases de educación vial y manejo supervisado.
2. Respuestas posibles: El poder se divide en tres ramas; las legislaturas son generalmente bicamerales (con una Cámara de Representantes y un Senado); hay un jefe del ejecutivo; hay tribunales de primera instancia y tribunales de apelación.
3. Las asambleas legislativas ciudadanas sólo se reúnen cada año por medio por un período de aproximadamente dos meses, mientras que las legislaturas profesionales se llevan a cabo anualmente y duran la mayor parte del año.

Teacher Management System

4. permitir al gobernador rechazar algunas partes de una ley pero aprobar el resto del proyecto
5. Respuesta posible: Un comité no partidista compila una lista de candidatos y el gobernador nombra juez a una persona de esa lista. En la siguiente elección, los votantes pueden elegir al mismo juez o reemplazarlo por otro.

SECCIÓN 3

Tomar notas

Las respuestas variarán.

Resumen de la sección

1. El gobierno de la ciudad emitió una moratoria para la construcción y después realizó audiencias y encargó un estudio para poder hallar las respuestas a las inquietudes de los residentes.
2. Respuesta posible: el gobierno municipal, ya que tendría más conocimiento de los problemas locales y sería potencialmente más accesible para los ciudadanos
3. regular el uso de la tierra
4. proponer y potencialmente hacer aprobar y promulgar una ley